LIVING BY DESIGN
Leslie Cheek and the Arts

LIVING BY DESIGN

LESLIE CHEEK AND THE ARTS

A Photobiography by Parke Rouse, Jr.

Foreword by John Walker
Afterword by John Canaday
Design by Raymond Geary

Published by
THE SOCIETY OF THE ALUMNI
of
THE COLLEGE OF WILLIAM AND MARY
Williamsburg, Virginia

First American Edition
Copyright © 1985 Society of the Alumni
College of William and Mary
Williamsburg, Virginia 23187

Grateful acknowledgment is made to the Virginia Museum of Fine Arts, Richmond, Virginia, for permission to reprint numerous photographs in their archives.

Library of Congress Card Catalogue Number: 85-73016

ISBN 0-9615670-0-7

Printed in Hong Kong by Overseas Color Printing Corporation, 6fl., 6 Des Voeux Road, Hong Kong

Dust jacket photograph: Leslie Cheek judging submissions to Ivan Dmitri's *Photography in the Fine Arts* at the 1964-65 New York World's Fair.

Dedicated to

Huldah Belle Warfield Wood
Mabel Wood Cheek
Mary Tyler Freeman Cheek
Elizabeth Tyler Cheek Morgan

Contents

Foreword

Leslie Cheek, in my opinion, is the most brilliant museum director of my generation. He took two moribund museums and made them exiting models for us all.

Basically, what he brought into the museum profession was a sense of drama. Fascinated by the theatre from an early age, he worked in it at Yale and elsewhere. He learned the importance of light in exhibitions, something art dealers have always known but curators had ignored. He used his knowledge to make the treasures he was showing dramatic and magnetic. To give the public a sense of the environment in which they were created, he brought in what are known in the theatre as "props." For example, to give the correct atmosphere for a show entitled *Modern Painting Isms and How They Grew,* he disguised a Baltimore Museum guard, gave him false whiskers and a frock coat to make him look like a French custodian of the 19th century. He placed him in attendance in a room suggesting a Louvre gallery filled with Salon paintings. But best of all the guard was encouraged, for time to time, to pinch a pretty visitor! This gave the scene its actuality and authenticity.

In another show, *Art Begins at Home,* he constructed a maze. At the entrance visitors were confronted by cubicles with two examples of various household furnishings—two alarm clocks, two radios, two teapots, etc.—and were told to select the one they thought better designed. Above each object was an arrow, which visitors were to follow after making a choice. If a poorly designed object were chosen, they ended up in a *cul-de-sac* with a label explaining why their choice was badly designed. Then they had to begin again. It took some people hours to get out of the show!

Such exhibitions were not only imaginative and innovative, but also laborious to put on. A member of Leslie's staff eventually came to work for me at the National Gallery of Art. She said Leslie was a slave driver, but she loved him. Had she gone on in Baltimore, however, she thought she would have a nervous breakdown. She felt she needed the calm of my museum to recuperate. Needless to say, I did not consider her remarks a compliment.

When war came, Leslie resigned from the Baltimore Museum and entered the Corps of Engineers. He was never made to be a subordinate bureaucrat, and that is what the Army tried to make him. But even so, he had his successes. Given an opportunity to lecture about camouflage, he started a course called "Conceal or Reveal." To keep his audience awake when he talked and showed slides, he mixed in with his conventional slides, a number showing a model named Chili Williams. A voluptuous girl, she appeared with as few clothes on as the Corps of Engineers would permit. His classroom had standing room only. For the students who had attained the highest marks, Major Cheek passed out glossy photographs of Chili and good cigars.

After two years at Fort Belvoir, its most popular Major was ordered to the Office of Strategic Services. He was to have been attached to the staff of Lord Louis Mountbatten to teach his native troops camouflage, but the project was called off. On the whole his time with the OSS was wasted.

Leslie had graduated from the Yale Architecture School and could have been a full-time practicing architect, and I feel sure he would have made an admirable one. But when the war ended he was offered an editorship on *Architectural Forum.* He thought he was to be a kind of deputy publisher. This did not work out; and though he loved his contacts with architects, he felt he needed more scope for his talents.

In 1948 he was offered the job of director of the Virginia Museum of Fine Arts. He went to Richmond to see what it looked like. It was dirty, needed refurbishing, and had had less and less impact on the community. The museum, only a fourth the size of the one he had headed in Baltimore, offered him the magnificent salary of $7,500, less than we paid our guards at the National Gallery of Art. But Leslie looked on it as a challenge, the greatest he faced; and because of his family's wealth, money did not matter.

One of his best exhibitions was *Sport and the Horse,* held in 1960. Paul Mellon was a trustee of the museum and Leslie asked him to be chairman of the show. Paul discussed the offer with me and felt reluctant to accept, saying he knew too little about English collections of any kind, but he admitted he knew the owners of paintings and might therefore be helpful to the Virginia Museum. Finally he decided to take the job provided he was given as his deputy an authority on English pictures. Basil Taylor was chosen, and the relationship was a long and fruitful one.

The exhibition was an overwhelming success. Paul became more and more enthusiastic about English painting, which he had never collected, though he owned a few examples. As a result of Leslie's show, Yale University now has its Center for British Art, a building erected with funds provided by Paul Mellon, and filled with the greatest collection in the world of British painting outside of the Tate Gallery in London.

The friendship of Paul Mellon and Leslie Cheek has been of extraordinary benefit to Richmond and to Virginia. The museum which, when Leslie arrived, was seedy and run down, is now among the most vital in the United States. Paul Mellon provided funds to carry out Leslie's dream of bringing art to small communities. To do this Leslie designed and had built an Artmobile. It was popular and its exhibitions gratefully welcomed wherever shown. Paul also gave a superb collection of French Impressionist pictures to the Virginia Museum to be placed in a new $22 million West Wing, to which he and his wife Rachel, along with Sydney and Frances Lewis of Richmond, and the Commonwealth of Virginia contributed.

Leslie Cheek's life has been one of magnificent achievement. I am delighted that it has now been recorded. All of us, especially those who are in the museum profession, can usefully read this book and learn from it. Leslie's imagination, determination and originality have had an impact on museums that will long outlast his generation.

—John Walker
London, England

Acknowledgements

The research for this book involved not only the author but three interviewers and researchers. They were K. Richmond Temple of Richmond, who interviewed many people and searched many files, including those of Leslie Cheek, Jr.; Mrs. Helen Stuhler Dohn of Richmond, who was secretary to Mr. Cheek during his latter years at the Virginia Museum; and Mrs. Elizabeth Cheek Morgan of Belmont, Massachusetts, who interviewed some of her father's former associates in the early stages of this project. Richmond Temple has worked valiantly to coordinate the project and get it to press, including editing and proofing the text, and writing all captions.

The author is also greatly indebted to Mrs. Dorothy Saunders Nielsen, Mr. Cheek's secretary since 1969, who with Richmond Temple handled much of the correspondence.

Among the many people interviewed by the author, he is especially indebted to Paul Mellon of Upperville; J. Carter Brown, director of the National Gallery of Art, Washington; Leonard Haber of New York; Clyde Newhouse of Newhouse Galleries, New York; Robert Stewart of Richmond; Thomas Craven of Charlottesville; Mrs. Muriel Branham Christison of Williamsburg; Glenn Lowry of Washington; and Pinkney Near of Richmond.

Other information was provided by Mrs. Florence Knoll Bassett of Coconut Grove, Florida; Alistair Cooke of New York; Bernard Bothmer of New York University, New York; Vincent Price of Los Angeles; Roger Mudd of Washington; Mrs. Huldah Cheek Sharp of Brentwood, Tennessee; Leslie Cheek III of Washington; Richard Cheek of Belmont, Massachusetts; Thomas Messer, director of the Guggenheim Museum, New York; G. E. Kidder Smith of New York; Russell Lynes of North Egremont, Massachusetts; Lewis Mumford of Amenia, New York; Robert Telford of Long Beach, California; John Döepp of Brunswick, Maine; Vincent Bowditch of Kailua, Hawaii; Miss Margaret Powell of Baltimore; Frank McCarthy of Beverly Hills, California; William Ryan of Richmond; David Hudson of Kansas City, Missouri; Guy Friddell of Norfolk; David Yerkes of Washington; Miss Betty Stacy of Richmond; David Bradley of Richmond; Mrs. Marian Friedman Winer of Richmond, Lee Powers of Lake Lure, North Carolina; William Morrison of Washington; Perry Rathbone of New York; Mrs. Margaret Dodge Garrett of Washington; Mrs. Adelyn Dohme Breeskin of Washington; Mrs. Swepson Earle of Baltimore; and Mrs. Mary Moore Jacoby of Richmond.

Also Mrs. Mae Wright Reid of Newark, Delaware; Edwin Yoder of Richmond; Philip Johnson of New York; Raymond Geary of Richmond; Mrs. Monica Scanlon Hamm of Richmond; Richard Woodward of Richmond; Ronald Jennings of Richmond; Edward Gill of Richmond; Dennis McWaters of Crozier; Frederick Brandt of Richmond; Hansford Rowe of New York; Robert and Elodie Osborn of Salisbury, Connecticut; Lester Lamb of Tenafly, New Jersey; Edwin Rust of Memphis, Tennessee; James Cogar of Midway, Kentucky; Richard Washburn of Lake Lure, North Carolina; Mrs. Marian Hinman Gracey of Hampton; Miss Kay Murphy Halle of Washington; James Fitch of New York; Norris Houghton of New York; Thomas Howe of San Francisco, California; Mrs. Edith Thacher Hurd of Mill Valley, California; and Lincoln Kirstein of New York.

Also, Sherman Lee of Chapel Hill, North Carolina; Carl Weinhardt, Jr., director of the Frederick Bartlett Museum, Fort Lauderdale, Florida; Anthony Zanghi of New York, Daniel Reeves of Madison, Tennessee; William O'Neal of Charlottesville; Frederick Nichols of Charlottesville; Otto Wittmann of Malibu, California; William Gaines of Dunnsville; Lowell and Viola Humphreys of Vesuvius; Rear Admiral Thomas and Sophie Bass of Stratford; David Payne of Newport, Rhode Island; Paul Grotz of New York, William Bailey of Lynchburg; Dr. John Ashworth of Richmond; Mrs. Tweet Kimball of Sedalia, Colorado; Ariel Baillif of Salt Lake City, Utah; Conley Edwards of Richmond; Mrs. Muriel Matier Quinn of Williamsburg; Mrs. Annemarie Pope, president, International Exhibition Foundation, Washington; Mrs. James Rorimer of New York; Gordon Bunschaft of New York; and James Whitehead, Washington and Lee University, Lexington.

Among those interviewed or assisting in Richmond were Benjamin and Frances Lambert, Mrs. Edith Lindeman Calisch, Jon Longaker, Mrs. Lucy Harvey Sydnor, Mrs. Laila Wheary Pearsall, Mrs. Martha Orr Davenport, Mrs. Jacquelin Wolnan Viener, Mrs. Janet Billet Kennedy, Mrs. Frances Richardson Shield, Mrs. Sarah Keyser Starke, Mrs. Frances Boushall Valentine, Mrs. Anne Hobson Freeman, William Rhodes, Jr., Richard Velz, Paul N. Perrot, director of the Virginia Museum, Oliver Sands, Jr., D. Tennant Bryan, Mrs. Mary Taylor Robertson, C. Willard Alley, G. Mallory Freeman, Harry Robertson III, William Bradley and John Bradley.

Among the institutions which provided data or illustrations were the Boston Museum of Fine Art, the Museum of Modern Art, the Metropolitan Historical Commission of Nashville, the Virginia State Library, the Virginia Museum, the U.S. Army Engineers' Museum, Stratford Hall Plantation, Rockefeller Center, Inc., the Virginia Historical Society, Christie's, the Baltimore Museum of Art, the College of William and Mary, and Washington and Lee University.

The author appreciates the valued co-operation of Leslie and Mary Tyler Cheek during the creation of this book in the years 1984 and 1985.

—P.R., JR.

The pineapple design in this book was created by Leslie Cheek in the 1930s, when his mother asked him to style some stationery for her use at Cheek-wood. Later, in emulation of his ancestors who had small pineapples placed on their carriages, Cheek had this traditional symbol of hospitality attached to the doors of his automobiles.

Pumpkin with a Stable-Lad, by George Stubbs, 1774. Paul Mellon Collection, Upperville, Virginia.

14

CHAPTER I

Renaissance in Richmond

The dinner at the formal preview for *Sport and the Horse* was held in the Virginia Museum's Medieval Hall on the evening of April 2, 1960. The Earl of Halifax (standing at the rostrum at center), Chairman of the Masters of Foxhounds Association of England, was the main speaker at the gala opening of the internationally-acclaimed exhibition.

The Virginia Museum had never invited a more glittering throng than the one which gathered in the Medieval Hall on the evening of April 2, 1960. The elegantly attired crowd had gathered for the Sponsors' Dinner at the opening of *Sport and the Horse,* the museum's international exhibition dedicated to sporting art. The ambassadors of France and Great Britain, both exhibition patrons, were present. Guests converged at the receiving line to exchange pleasantries with the guests of honor, the Earl and Countess of Halifax. Also with them were Virginia's Governor and Mrs. J. Lindsay Almond, Jr., museum president and Mrs. John Garland Pollard, Jr., and Mr. and Mrs. Paul Mellon. Mr. Mellon was organizing chairman for *Sport and the Horse.*

The final couple in the receiving line was Leslie Cheek, Jr., director of the museum, and his wife, Mary Tyler.

This evening one could not help but notice Cheek, the museum's director since 1948. He had an intensity about him, and even as he pumped outstretched hands and chatted with guests, he seemed acutely aware of everything going on around him. As well he should, since this premiere culminated nearly two years of planning, and he wanted every detail executed without mishap. Indeed, earlier in the day, before he went home to change into formal attire, he had, with characteristic thoroughness, inspected the seating and place-settings at each banquet table. *Sport and the Horse* would put the Virginia Museum on the national cultural map as an institution of significance.

When he came to the museum twelve years earlier, he had done so with the idea of improving the cultural climate of Virginia, and of the South in general, which due to its defeated Confederacy and agrarian economy, had not had the opportunity to cultivate the fine arts. Cheek, a Tennessean by birth, wanted to show the American museum world how far the South had come.

The idea for an exhibition dedicated to the world's finest horse paintings had been born in the late 1940s. Asa Shield, a museum trustee and master of Richmond's Deep Run Hunt, had suggested the idea to Cheek, but a lack of funds then made it impossible to mount such an exhibit.

In his first decade as director, Cheek sought to animate the museum, to expand its programs; and, more importantly, obtain increased private support—essential if the museum were to grow. During the 1950s, as he staged a series of exhibitions remarkable for their breadth, from architecture to photography to fashion, and for the unforgettable manner in which they were displayed—Leslie never forgot about Shield's proposal.

The receiving line at the preview for *Sport and the Horse.* Leslie Cheek (left) stands next to Mrs. Mellon (center) and Mr. Mellon (right). Mr. Mellon served as organizing chairman of the exhibition.

Mrs. John Garland Pollard, Jr., (whose husband was president of the Virginia Museum at the time of *Sport and the Horse*), Dr. James Asa Shield, and Mary Tyler Cheek. In the late 1940s Dr. Shield, a noted Virginia horseman, first proposed a museum exhibition entirely devoted to equestrian art.

Paul Mellon, the Virginia Museum's greatest benefactor.

Cheek sought to interest well-to-do Virginians in the future of the museum. Among those whose aid he sought was Paul Mellon, of Upperville, the son of Andrew Mellon, the financier who had founded the National Gallery in Washington in the 1930s. Paul Mellon had been born and reared in Pittsburgh, but had chosen to live in Virginia's hunt country after graduating from Yale and Cambridge University in England. Following World War II he set up his Old Dominion Foundation in Washington to support the arts and humanities, chiefly in his new home state. He devoted himself to raising and racing thoroughbred horses at his Rokeby Stables near Upperville.

Mellon and Cheek first met at a Virginia Museum trustees meeting in 1948. The two, who were almost the same age, had much in common. Each was the son of a wealthy father, and each had studied at Yale. Both had served in the Office of Strategic Services in

World War II. The two had decided to involve themselves in the arts, rather than in a family business.

J. Carter Brown, director of the National Gallery of Art, once observed that "A regional museum by nature must depend heavily on borrowed materials and visiting exhibitions. But every museum must have its own collection—must have things it can lend if it expects to borrow. Leslie Cheek went after Paul Mellon's help with its art. Mellon credits Leslie Cheek and the Virginia Museum with getting his collecting juices going."

Much of Leslie Cheek's success at the Virginia Museum was due to the involvement of Paul Mellon and other collectors. His zeal was contagious.

When construction began in 1951 on the museum's new Theatre Wing, director Cheek turned to the Old Dominion Foundation for half the project's $2 million cost. Mellon often lent the museum objects from his private collection, such as sculptures by Edgar Degas in 1956.

In 1958 when the idea for a sporting art exhibition resurfaced, Cheek asked Mellon if he would serve as chairman of an international exhibition to be called, *Sport and the Horse*. It was an apt choice, since Mellon's involvement with horse breeding and racing extended beyond American shores to England and the continent. He knew many of the English families who owned horse paintings which the museum would seek to borrow for the proposed exhibition. Luckily for the museum and the art world, Paul Mellon accepted. He generously offered to cover the cost of any deficit which the museum might incur in mounting such a lavish exhibition. He would later acknowledge that his chairmanship of *Sport and the Horse* stimulated his collecting of English paintings, a passion which would benefit the Virginia Museum, Yale University and the National Gallery.

In the summer of 1958 Cheek decided the show should open with great fanfare in the spring of 1960, to coincide with Virginia's steeplechase season. He also organized a selection committee to include himself, John Walker, then director of the National Gallery, Andrew Ritchie, head of the Yale University Art Gallery, and W. G. Constable, formerly curator with the Boston Museum of Fine Arts. The fifth member was an Englishman, Basil Taylor, librarian at London's Royal College of Art, an authority on the paintings of George Stubbs, the 19th century British artist whose works would be the centerpiece of *Sport and the Horse*. Since so many of the best horse paintings hung in the homes of the English aristocracy, Taylor could not only recommend which paintings ought to be included in the exhibition, but would also know their whereabouts.

Further research was provided by the Virginia Museum's associate director Muriel Christison, and curator, Pinkney Near. In January of 1959 they travelled to New York to meet with W. G. Constable. During this conference the basic form which the exhibition would ultimately assume was set. Constable recommended that Stubbs' works be at the heart of *Sport and the Horse*. He also urged Christison and Near to include the works of other horse painters like Gilpin, Marshall, Seymour, and Wootton. Above all, the bulk of the exhibition should come from abroad. Britain's Tate Gallery should be asked for a loan, and Paul Mellon should approach Sir Anthony Blunt, Surveyor of the Queen's Collection, to seek the loan of a painting from Queen Elizabeth II.

Cheek endorsed all these proposals, and added one of his own. Several years before, when the museum presented *Design in Scandinavia*, President Eisenhower and the heads of state of the four foreign nations participating had served as patrons for the exhibition. Cheek decided a similar approach for *Sport and the Horse* would be appropriate, and would lend prestige to both the show and the museum. It was agreed that President Eisenhower, Queen Elizabeth II, and President DeGaulle of France would be asked to be honorary patrons.

For help in this matter, Cheek wrote Walter S. Robertson, a Richmonder and vice-president of the museum, who was then an Assistant Secretary of State. "We have employed special expert advisers both here and in England, and have now reached the point where certain major English and French loans must be requested," Cheek told Robertson. "In each case, backing from our State Department will be needed, but in different ways. In England we are already in direct contact with Sir Anthony Blunt, Surveyor of the Queen's Collection, and other key lenders, most of whom prefer informal personal negotiations before official letters are exchanged . . ."

Cheek asked Robertson to get backing from U.S. ambassadors Amory Houghton in France, and John Hay Whitney in Great Britain. Cheek had served with Whitney on the Yale Council. He also asked Robertson to contact someone on the White House staff to approach the President about being a patron.

Walter S. Robertson (left) and Leslie Cheek confer in the director's office at the Virginia Museum. As Assistant Secretary of State, Robertson used his influence to enlist President Dwight D. Eisenhower as an Honorary Patron for *Sport and the Horse*. Britain's Queen Elizabeth II was also an Honorary Patron. Robertson later served as president of the museum from 1960 to 1967, the period during which the state-supported art institution experienced unprecedented growth.

The Earl Fitzwilliam lent *Mares and Foals* to the Virginia Museum for *Sport and the Horse*, one of twelve paintings by George Stubbs to appear in the exhibition.

Lewis Strauss, Secretary of Commerce-designate, and a Virginian who was a museum trustee, was also enlisted to approach the President. Leslie felt that if Eisenhower's consent could be gained first, then the Queen and DeGaulle would follow suit.

Meanwhile, Mrs. Christison had been writing dozens of letters to potential lenders in England. At first, the responses were disappointing. Sir John Rothenstein, director of London's Tate Gallery, wrote he could not lend two paintings requested by the museum, since one was on loan and the other could not leave its special gallery. Other refusals came from several noble families, including the Earl of Spencer, whose daughter, Diana, would later marry Prince Charles.

News from France was equally disheartening. The Louvre in Paris voiced its reluctance to lend a much-wanted race horse painting by Théodore Géricault, entitled *Epsom Downs Derby.*

Cheek, however, was persistent. In the spring 1959 he resolved to go to England and France himself to break the logjam, booked passage on a trans-Atlantic liner, and arrived in England during the last week of April. During his two-week stay overseas, Leslie sought the loan of twenty top horse paintings. Ambassador Whitney had, at Cheek's request, written a dozen prospective lenders, and he had even agreed to lend two of his own paintings. Whitney's groundwork proved helpful, and Cheek found the British owners generally receptive.

In Paris, however, the museum's impresario found the French more aloof. Before flying home, Cheek visited Edmond Sidet, director of the Louvre, with whom he discussed the loan of the Géricault. He reminded Sidet that the Virginia Museum had recently lent a Poussin to the Louvre, and hoped that the French would reciprocate. Despite these entreaties, Monsieur Sidet remained noncommital.

In Paris, ambassador Amory Houghton was diligently seeking DeGaulle's consent, but *le grand Charles* would not budge. The museum dealt with the Louvre through Houghton's assistant, Joseph Verner Reed. Many weeks after Cheek's visit, Reed was still wrangling with the bureaucracy, trying to nail down the Géricault loan. It was a frustrating affair. Reed wrote Cheek that "I am so sick of the whole business I would like to shove the Géricault in their faces." He nevertheless assured the museum that he would stick to the "ridiculous quest."

Meanwhile, the Virginia Museum was trying to line up American lenders. In June 1959, Leslie provided Paul Mellon a list of fifteen potential sources. Mellon found his own name on the list, as well as the National Gallery in Washington, the Jockey Club of New York, Harvard's Fogg Art Museum, Colonial Williamsburg Foundation, the Chicago Art Institute, and Baltimore's Walters Gallery.

In July of 1959, Cheek, joined by his wife, Mary Tyler, sailed back to Europe on the S.S. *United States.* His ostensible mission was to attend an International Committee of Museums meeting in Stockholm and to advise a committee in Dunfermline, Scotland which wanted to establish a museum honoring native son Andrew Carnegie. However, Cheek had written ahead to Basil Taylor in London that "we might stop at the country estate of one or two key lenders . . ."

While at sea, Cheek spoke by radio-telephone with Joseph Reed in Paris. The connection was poor, but he was able to hear Reed say the request to President DeGaulle had been lost "somewhere in the Quai d'Orsai."

Leslie had better luck with the French when he reached Stockholm, for he found the Louvre's Edmond Sidet also at the ICOM meeting. He and Cheek met at a reception given the participants by Swedish King Gustav VI, at historic Drottningholm Palace. Before the day was over the Virginia Museum had been given the Louvre's assurances that it would loan a Géricault.

In England, Cheek met with Basil Taylor, and the two talked about the catalogue for the exhibition which Taylor was to write, and they discussed which English lender ought to be

Leslie and Mary Tyler Cheek on board the *S.S. United States,* enroute to Europe, July 1959.

Cheek (right) confers with Basil Taylor, at that time the world's leading authority on George Stubbs.

La Course, by Theodore Géricault, lent by the Musée du Louvre, Paris.

invited to the museum as the guest of honor. Taylor suggested that the Earl of Rosebery, a leading sportsman and collector, might consent. Cheek's English host described the Earl as "a key figure" with "a unique place . . . in . . . sporting and art circles of the English aristocracy."

Throughout the summer and fall of 1959 efforts to involve President DeGaulle in *Sport and the Horse* continued. In September of that year, Assistant Secretary Robertson approached French Foreign Minister Couve de Murville at the United Nations in New York, but learned that de Murville knew nothing of the matter. The austere Frenchman added discouragingly that DeGaulle had "never done anything like this before" and he doubted the French President would do so now. Sure enough, Joseph Reed wrote from Paris shortly thereafter that his office "had finally gotten word from reliable, highly placed sources that DeGaulle will refuse." He added, "A long way 'round the Mulberry Bush for a simple no."

With the President and Queen as honorary patrons, however, the museum assembled a list of patrons, headed by Virginia's Governor J. Lindsay Almond, Jr. This group included the British and French ambassadors to the United States, and the American ambassadors in London and Paris. Prince Aly Khan, then permanent representative of Pakistan to the United Nations was also a patron. He lent a painting, *A Skewbald Stallion*, by James Ward, to the exhibit.

As the opening date of the exhibition approached, Cheek and his staff had promises of 68 masterpieces. Although some requests had been declined, Cheek had handily exceeded his goal of 60 pictures, most of them never before exhibited to the public. Fifty-three were by the British artists Sawrey Gilpin, Ben Marshall, James Seymour, George Stubbs, James Ward and John Wootton. Ten works were by six French painters, Honoré Daumier, Alfred Dedreux, Edgar Degas, Jean-Louis Forain, Théodore Géricault, and Édouard Manet. Five were by the Swiss-born

The Races at Longchamp, Paris, by Édouard Manet, lent by the Art Institute of Chicago.

painter Edward Troye, who emigrated to Kentucky in the early 1830s. Troye was chosen to represent horse painting in America.

The museum was ecstatic when notified Queen Elizabeth II was lending two paintings by Gilpin and Marshall, one from Windsor Castle, the other from Buckingham Palace. The Louvre finally came through with Géricault's masterful *La Course*.

For the exhibition, Cheek designed a special series of galleries, the entrances for which were decorated with arches upholstered in "pink" satin in the spirit of the occasion. Each room presented the equestrian art from either France, England or America. The hardbound, illustrated catalogue was designed by Yale's Alvin Eisenman and won a "Book of the Year" citation in 1961.

When the display opened, it aroused enthusiastic notice from the public and the press. Since most of the works had never

before been exhibited publicly, they were especially noteworthy. *Time* magazine carried an account, and critics came from New York and Washington. One account in the *Richmond Times-Dispatch* reported:

Leslie Cheek Junior's luggage and shoe leather got a workout in the past year of preparations . . . Cheek traveled to Europe twice in his search for top examples of sporting art from Britain, France, and America. He saw ambassadors, art authorities, and collectors on both sides of the Atlantic. Before he was through, Cheek had hiked to a few remote castles to borrow canvasses that had hung on the same walls since they were painted more than 100 years ago . . .

The star of the show was clearly George Stubbs, whose critical recognition as the most masterful of all English animal painters was firmly established by the Virginia Museum's

ABOVE: Stubbs' *Hambletonian, Rubbing Down* (lent by the Estate of the Marchioness Dowager of Londonderry) dominated the gallery which featured English sporting art. Two other galleries were for French and American loans. **RIGHT:** Cheek's installation for the exhibit featured walls covered with satin in the "pink" hue favored by mounted huntsmen. Note the explanatory text beneath the entrance sign to the exhibition. Cheek's object was to engage the mind while delighting the eye of every museum visitor.

show and Basil Taylor's research. "The more I saw of Stubbs, the more I became enamored of his work," Cheek told *Life* magazine writer Dorothy Sieberling shortly before the exhibition opened. "I had long thought of Stubbs only as a 'horse painter,' and now feel that he is one of the major artists of the English School of the 18th century."

"The exhibition they [Cheek and Mellon] mounted in Richmond in 1961 proved to be as important for the appreciation of British painting in this country as was the Armory Show in 1913 for the Post-Impressionists," wrote John Walker, former director of the National Gallery, in his autobiography, *Self-Portrait with Donors.* "After the Virginia Museum exhibition, American collectors had a new respect for the creativity of British artists."

As a result of his role in the exhibition, Paul Mellon began acquiring English paintings which he was later to give to Yale University, the National Gallery in Washington, and the Virginia Museum. With the advice of Basil Taylor, Mellon assembled over 400 British masterpieces of the 18th and 19th centuries. Just three years after *Sport and the Horse* closed, the Virginia Museum would present *Painting in England,* the first public display of Mellon's new English collection. Every gallery in the museum was used to house this mammoth exhibition, which ran from April to August, 1963.

Recalling *Sport and the Horse* two decades after it had been held, Mellon gave Cheek credit for having made the Virginia Museum one of the country's most vital art institutions. "Undoubtedly in his years as director . . . Leslie Cheek was a very great asset to the Virginia Museum," he said, "but people don't realize how great. *Sport and the Horse* was an eye-opener about English pictures to people in the United States. Leslie had a great flair for making things look well. He got me interested in the museum in the first place. When I began to know him, the Old Dominion Foundation was just getting underway. Leslie was interested in building a theatre wing on the

Charles Campbell and His Brothers, by Sawrey Gilpin, lent by the Lord Emlyn. Gilpin was one of six British artists honored in the exhibition.

museum, and more exhibition space. I was able to help with those."

Continuing to serve as a Virginia Museum trustee, Mellon proceeded to add richly to its collections. In 1962 he provided funds to construct Artmobile II. Later he would give the museum an extensive collection of French Impressionist paintings, to be displayed in a new $22 million wing to which he and Sydney and Frances Lewis contributed. This new West Wing, scheduled to open in December, 1985 will secure the Virginia Museum's reputation as an art center of international significance.

More Mellon gifts will be forthcoming in the future. "I've always been interested in country life," Paul Mellon confessed in 1983. "That partly explains why I live in Upperville, which is much like England. That is why I'm planning to give quite a few English sporting pictures to the Virginia Museum. We should have things in the museum that relate to the English heritage."

Sport and the Horse established Leslie Cheek as one of America's most imaginative and energetic museum directors. During his twenty years at the Virginia Museum—from 1948 to 1968—he guided it to unprecedented growth in its collections, its talented staff, and its physical plant. During his tenure, he showed the world how a small, but well-run museum could stimulate the arts in a region which before the twentieth century had lacked the leisure or wealth to cultivate them.

When Carter Brown, director since 1969 of the National Gallery of Art in Washington, was a graduate student at New York University in 1952, he chose the Virginia Museum as the subject of his term paper. In it he wrote that Cheek's "very innovative, very dynamic programs opened almost a new chapter in the way American museums operate."

In his two decades as head of the nation's first statewide art museum program, Cheek fought many battles. He was determined that the arts should assume a wider role in the life of the Commonwealth. He helped lead art institutions in Virginia and in the South to reach the standards of such well-established museums as those in Boston, New York and Washington—all founded in the two-year period 1869 and 1870—when the South was demoralized by Reconstruction.

No wonder Brown hailed the Virginia Museum under Cheek's leadership as "the most interesting in America," and that he regarded its creation of local chapters, served by Artmobiles and travelling exhibitions, as "a kind of microcosm of the way the National Gallery now serves the country."

"Leslie Cheek impressed me tremendously by his interest in the way works of art should be displayed, the educational aspect of showing them, and the emphasis he put on the spruceness of the building," Carter Brown added. "I also admire the unique combining of the performing arts with the others making the museum into a cultural center. In so many ways it was a forward-looking place. Mr. Cheek was very exacting, very demanding of his staff, which was hard on some of them some of the time, but he managed to get things done. He was terrific at planning. He was always working things out way in advance, right down to the smallest detail."

Most of all, Brown was impressed by his colleague's sense of design—a passion that had animated Leslie Cheek from his youth in Nashville through a career in teaching fine arts, in designing buildings and stage sets, and in giving life to art museums. "Leslie lives in a visual world," the National Gallery director concluded. "Everything in his world had to do with design: labels, galleries, structures, and the rest."

Above all else, Leslie Cheek sought to make life harmonious and beautiful through his sense of design. Through exhibitions like *Sport and the Horse* and in countless other ways, he helped his contemporaries to see and enjoy the arts. The Cheek era will be remembered as a time of exhilaration in Virginia. Truly, he made his artistic vision contagious. ☐

The Boulevard façade of the Virginia Museum of Fine Arts, April 1960. French and British flags flew from twelve flagpoles, and heralded one of the museum's most important exhibitions. The banners and colorful outdoor signs were among the many innovations introduced by Leslie Cheek during his twenty-year directorship.

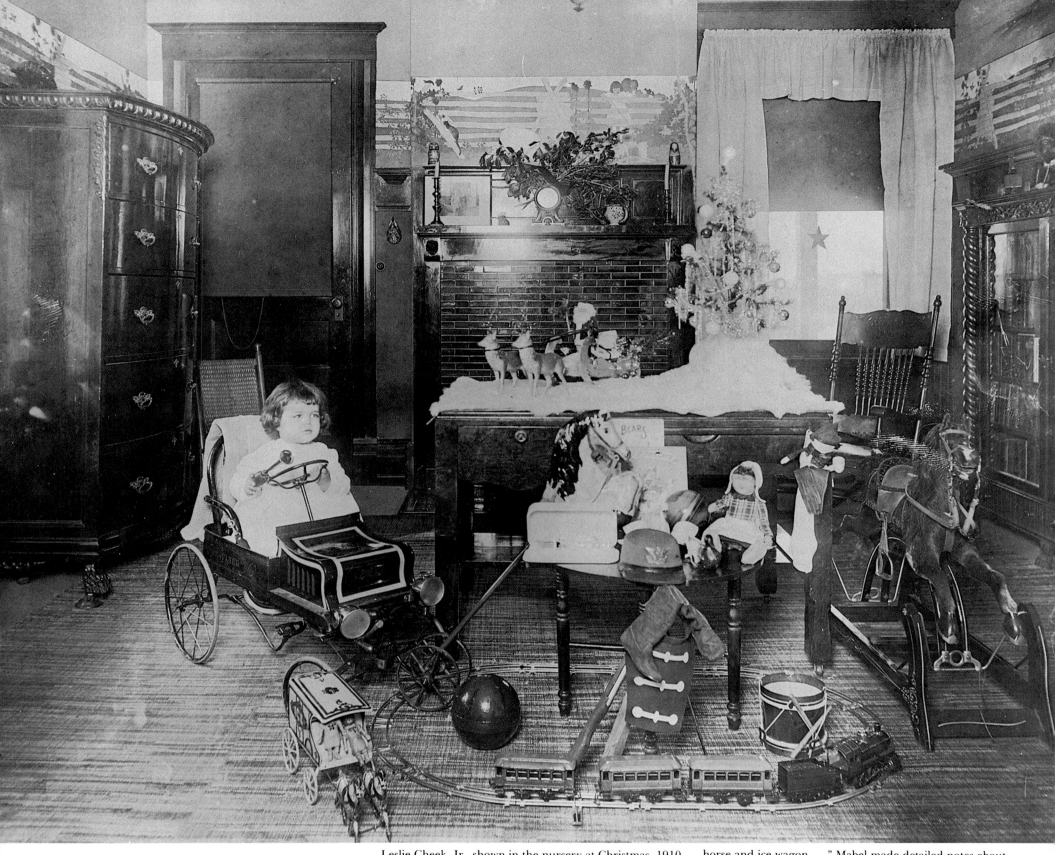

Leslie Cheek, Jr., shown in the nursery at Christmas, 1910. His mother, Mabel Wood Cheek, noted in her family album that "the toys he most enjoyed were the automobile, hobby horse and ice wagon . . ." Mabel made detailed notes about her son's every activity and interest from his youth to adulthood.

CHAPTER II

The Cheeks of Tennessee

Nashville in 1900 was one of the rising cities of the 20th century South. Despite the ravages of the Civil War and Reconstruction, it had become the centerpiece of a centennial in 1897, celebrating one hundred years of Tennessee statehood. A replica of the Greek Parthenon was built for the occasion in a special park. Vanderbilt University, endowed by Cornelius Vanderbilt and opened in 1875 as a symbol of Southern resurgence, gave prestige to the city, which called itself "The Athens of the South."

No family was more a part of Nashville's growth in these years than the Cheeks. Joel Cheek had started a wholesale grocery business in Nashville after the Reconstruction, developing a coffee blend he had adroitly named for the Maxwell House, a celebrated Nashville hotel. The business prospered. In 1890 Joel persuaded his first cousin, Christopher Tompkins Cheek, to move from Kentucky and head the grocery firm so that Joel could give full time to expanding Maxwell House Coffee's national market.

Christopher's son, Preston Leslie Cheek, became a partner in the Cheek grocery firm in 1895, and succeeded his father as president in 1915. He also had a large interest in the Cheek-Neal Coffee Company that made Maxwell House, and was involved in banking. By 1915 the fortunes of super-salesman Joel Cheek and of his cousin Leslie were clearly on the rise.

Nashville remembers Preston Leslie Cheek's family as a remarkable one. They lived in style, enjoying world travel and the arts at a time when most Americans had neither the time nor taste for trans-oceanic crossings. When Cheek built his first house in 1900 on Nashville's wide West End Avenue, across from the Vanderbilt campus, he and his wife chose a luxurious Italianate design. Many of the town fathers lived on that avenue, where trolley cars brought Vanderbilt students and black cooks from across town each morning.

Into the Cheek household was born, on

A full-size replica of the historic Greek Parthenon was built in Nashville for the 1897 Tennessee Centennial. (Courtesy: Metropolitan Historical Commission, Nashville)

Leslie Cheek, Sr., built this Italianate-style house near the Vanderbilt University campus in 1900. The design was suggested by his wife Mabel.

October 28, 1908, a first child. He was named Leslie Cheek, Jr., omitting his father's first name, Preston, which had honored his father's maternal grandfather, Preston Leslie, a two-term governor of early Kentucky, and, by appointment of President Cleveland, governor of the Montana territory.

Young Leslie remained an only child for six years, until a sister, Huldah was born in 1914. They were to be the only children of their parents and the darlings of their grandmothers. One was the tiny and energetic Huldah Belle Warfield Wood, the mother of Mabel Cheek, who lived with her daughter and son-in-law. The other grandmother, equally affectionate but less accessible, was Ann Leslie Cheek.

Little Leslie grew up at the center of this close and admiring family. Old-fashioned black servants, who lived on the premises, cushioned the Cheeks' lives. Blue-eyed, handsome Leslie was the idol of his nurse, Florence Drake, whom everyone called "Mammy." Her son, Ed Drake, chauffeured father Cheek downtown to work each day, and fetched him back home for a long lunch every afternoon. Also working in the house were the cook, Mary Lou, and a gardener, Emilio, who doubled as a butler. A housemaid, laundress and servingmen came in as needed.

But the dominant force in little Leslie's life was his vital mother, Mabel Wood Cheek. She was a matronly 34 when he was born. An only child, dynamic Mabel had been brought up by her parents in small town Tennessee luxury, but she preferred urban life. She was an avid reader and traveler, and she lived for the Metropolitan Opera's week-long visit to Nashville each spring. Mabel's contemporaries in Nashville's exclusive Centennial Club considered her a blue-stocking.

Her husband-to-be had first seen pretty young Mabel on a train in Kentucky. Smitten at first sight, Cheek had bribed the conductor with a box of cigars to learn the girl's name. Eighteen months later he had led her to the alter despite her prior engagement to another suitor.

Leslie Cheek, Jr.'s, great-grandfather, Preston H. Leslie (1819-1907) served as governor of Kentucky and later, by presidential appointment, of the Montana Territory. His daughter, Ann Valeria, married Christopher Tompkins Cheek, founder of a large southern wholesale grocery business, C. T. Cheek and Sons.

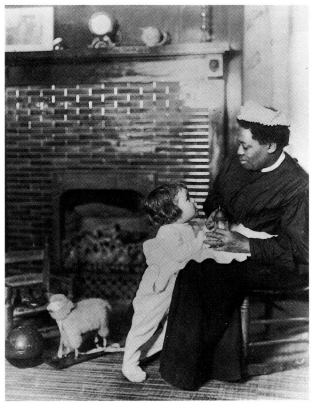

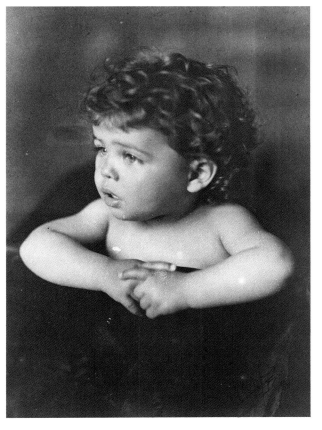

ABOVE RIGHT: Leslie, Jr., in the nursery at age two with devoted Mammy, Florence Drake. **RIGHT:** At twenty-one months his mother wrote of him, "A handsome specimen of a boy . . . His powers of imitation and gift of mimicry are wonderful. He is an impetuous, self-willed little creature and usually shows off beautifully for company."

31

LEFT: On October 3, 1896, twenty-two year old Mabel Wood of Clarksville, Tennessee, and Leslie Cheek, age twenty-four, of Nashville, were wed. He was already a managing partner in the wholesale grocery firm begun by his father, Christopher Tompkins Cheek.

BELOW: Four generations of Leslie Cheek's maternal ancestors gathered for this remarkable photograph taken around 1890. (Left to right) Leslie's great-great grandmother, Mary H. Boisseau; his mother, Mabel Wood; and her mother, Huldah Warfield Wood; and great-grandmother, Adelia Boisseau Warfield. **RIGHT:** William Wallace Warfield, Leslie's great-grandfather, is shown with his son, William, Jr. **FAR RIGHT:** Adelia Boisseau Warfield is depicted with daughter Huldah, who later married Louis Wood. These two portraits, which measure over seven feet tall, were painted around 1857 by American artist Robert Loftin Newman.

Highly disciplined herself, Mabel instilled lofty purpose in her son and her daughter from their first years. She accepted no less than their best efforts, chiding them if they fell below it. She gave them her taste for household luxury, for the arts, and for travel to exotic places. "My mother represented the gentler, intellectual character of her family," her son said many years later. She held up as examples the lives of her maternal grandparents, Adelia Boisseau and William Wallace Warfield, who went west from Maryland and Virginia in the early 1800s, when Tennessee was a new state. Their life-size portraits adorned the Cheeks' Nashville house.

If anything, Mabel was too protective of her children. She declined to send them to public schools, which she felt were too rough. She discouraged movies, but indulgent grandmother Huldah Warfield Wood occasionally took Leslie to a good one. Father Cheek risked his wife's disapproval by sometimes taking young Leslie to vaudeville held at the Princess Theatre on Friday night. As a part owner of the Princess, Cheek senior received free house seats that let him and his son happily watch from the balcony as jugglers, dancers, magicians and singers performed in turn. The shows were far from dazzling, but young Leslie grew to love the footlights.

ABOVE: A proud father holds his six-month-old son. Leslie Cheek, Sr., was a kindly man with a lively sense of humor. He enjoyed cigars, Vaudeville in Nashville's Princess Theatre and world travel. **RIGHT:** "Some fact or model was always impressed on his little mind." Mabel Cheek supervises little Leslie's reading in Nashville, ca. 1913. **FAR RIGHT:** Leslie's fascination with costumes, something that developed into a life-long passion, started early. Here, at age five, he models a Tyrolean outfit, which his grandmother Wood bought for him.

The Cheeks traveled frequently. In 1922 they toured Europe and in Granada, Spain, Leslie, fourteen, and Huldah, eight, posed in Arabic costume. Note the *trompe l'oeil* backdrop.

In 1926-27 the Cheeks went on an around-the-world tour. Beginning in the Far East they journeyed to Indo-China, India (where this photo was taken), then to Egypt, Turkey and Europe.

ABOVE RIGHT: This view of (left to right) Huldah, Mabel and Leslie Cheek, Sr., near the busy docks at Shanghai was made by Leslie Jr., with a movie camera. **RIGHT:** Father Cheek carefully weaves his way through a crowded bazaar in Shanghai.

Mabel Cheek took her children each spring to Nashville's Metropolitan Opera performances. She also led her family on far-ranging trips each summer to escape the Nashville heat. Within a year of Leslie's birth in 1908, she had taken him to Florida, Nova Scotia and to the resort town of Wequetonsing on the shore of Lake Michigan. In later summers she and her husband took the children to Sewanee in Tennessee, to the mountains of North Carolina and to Cape Cod.

In 1916, when Leslie was 8, Mabel and her husband took the boy on a tour of the far west. Two years later, in 1918, the family journeyed to New York, where it dutifully visited museums and theatres, and saw Uncle Will Cheek sail for World War I service in France. Gaining momentum, Mabel got Thomas Cook and Sons to work out globe-girdling trips to the Pacific Isles and the Orient in 1919, and to the British Isles and Europe three years later.

After each foray, knowledgeable Mabel brought her family and notebooks home and gave a travelogue on what she'd seen to the ladies of the Centennial Club. Then she would begin all over again to plan another trip, keeping Thomas Cook's Nashville office busy lining up ship, train and hotel accommodations for her family a full year in advance.

In 1925, gratified that Leslie shared her passion for travel, Mabel persuaded her husband to take a year away from his work and take the family on a trip around the world. They visited forbidden cities in China and spent nights with missionaries in lands that few westerners had then penetrated. From China, the Cheeks journeyed to Cambodia, India, Egypt, Turkey, Austria and France. To make a record of their travels, young Leslie was given a movie camera, then a novelty, and took many reels of film. When he got home, he carefully edited these, adding explanatory titles. Already he had developed a thoroughness and methodical approach which pleased his parents. His movies show a plump, determined Mabel blithely shepherding her family through dangerous-looking bazaars and street

In November, 1908, one-month-old Leslie joins his parents for his first automobile ride. Family chauffeur Ed Drake, Mammy's son, is at the wheel of the Stevens-Duryea. Mammy has a firm hold of little Leslie.

mobs, while her husband puffed amiably on his cigar, immaculate in a business suit and Homburg. Huldah, chronically embarrassed by her mother's old fashioned style of dress, usually lurked off-camera to the rear.

From her son's birth until she died in 1946, Mabel Cheek wrote down thousands of details in scrapbooks. She recorded Leslie's first steps at 16 months, his first words two months later, prep school honors, his marriage and his children. The young mother thought her baby remarkable at imitating sounds of animals and trains. In her scrapbook she noted that he liked blue bottles and "would amuse himself for hours with these things." Her obsession with her "beautiful baby" was touching, though it was to prove hard on her daughter Huldah.

When Mabel took little Leslie for his first drive in the family's handsome new Stevens-Duryea, driven by Ed Drake, a flat tire forced the passengers to return by trolley. "His fondness for automobiles still continued," Mabel noted, "and he enjoyed sitting in Ed's lap and assisting in running our machine, when he would imitate every movement made by Ed."

Young Leslie developed his mother's love for reading. When Mabel read bedtime stories she noticed that "some fact or model was always impressed on his little mind." And Mammy's versions of incidents from the Bible, like her account of the landing of "Nora's ark" on "Mount Alleyrat" as she phrased it, left the boy with unforgettable images from the scriptures. He always remembered the Gustave Doré scenes of hellfire and damnation from Mammy's well thumbed Bible.

From the first Leslie showed imagination. To his youthful mind, lightning was God's searchlight. Rain was His rainwagon, spilling water from heaven to earth. He loved the world of make-believe he found in books, on the stage and in the movies. When he was four he attended Ringling Brothers' Circus, where he "was carried away and laughed and applauded loudly," his mother wrote. "At this age it was wonderful to see his little mind unfold. His imagination is vivid, and it is a source of unceasing interest to watch him play." Mabel's pride was touching.

In 1914, when Leslie was six, his father bought Sycamore, a farm 25 miles from Nashville, and built Bird Song Cabin out of cedar logs. The comfortable summer house was designed by Mabel. For several summers she and the children vacationed there while her husband commuted to Nashville to work. Leslie Junior spent much of his time swimming in Sycamore Creek and playing games with sister Huldah and with little Herbert Andrews, the Negro cook's son.

Leslie was not given an allowance, but he was paid a small sum to shine his father's shoes or perform other regular chores. When he was 12, his father built a little country store for him at Sycamore, and stocked it with groceries and notions. It was a serious profit venture. The boy kept careful books of expenses and income, winding up with a small profit. Each Friday, Father Cheek would arrive from Nashville with a ten-gallon tub of ice cream, to be sold as five-cent cones and ten-cent dishes. Leslie paid Huldah to wash dishes. Once he saw his collies, Rob Roy and McGregor, licking unwashed plates, but he did not let his customers in on this company secret.

Teen-aged Leslie was also assigned by his father to assist in the annual inventory of the family's huge grocery warehouse, a task which took the boy up to ten days to complete. Located near the Louisville and Nashville Railway tracks, the warehouse was dusty and hot, but Leslie did his duty without complaint. At noon each day his father treated him to lunch in a railroad car which had been converted into a lunch counter, called a "dog wagon." There the youngster, hungry after a morning of counting barrels and crates, wolfed down a workingman's fare of hamburgers and cold milk.

As young Leslie grew older, he was often in the company of his amiable, easygoing father. They became close and devoted, though the elder Cheek soon recognized his son had little interest in the family's business holdings.

Leslie, nine, and little sister Huldah, three, photographed with their father at Sycamore, the family's summer home near Nashville, 1917.

LEFT: When his son was twelve, Cheek, Sr., put Leslie in charge of a small country store at their Sycamore country place. Here he learned the rudiments of business, while selling ice cream, chewing gum and sundries. It was a serious venture, and the boy kept a detailed account book. Though running the little store was fun, Leslie never was attracted to the commercial world. **BELOW:** Father Cheek had business cards like this printed in the summer of 1920 to help publicize his son's fledgling grocery store.

It never gets too hot for me to work. How about You?

"Service wiih a Smile"
Cold Drinks, Fruits, Picnic Supplies, Ice Cream
Sycamore Supply Co.
West End of Bridge
Leslie Cheek, Jr.
Owner and Manager
Solicits Your Patronage

For nearly thirty years, Cousin Joel Cheek (1852-1935) was a salesman for a Nashville grocery firm. After experimenting with different coffee blends, he perfected what became known as the Maxwell House brand. Leslie Cheek, Sr., invested in his cousin's lucrative business, thus securing the family's fortune. Maxwell House was sold to General Foods in 1928 for $42 million, just one year before the onset of the Great Depression.

Before 1928, the Cheek-Neal Company marketed the highly popular coffee blend named for the famed Nashville hotel depicted on its label. (Courtesy, Raymond Geary)

Indeed, the older Cheek saw that the family's fortunes would eventually permit his son and daughter to be independently wealthy, pursuing whatever careers appealed to them.

This was assured in 1928 when Joel Cheek sold Maxwell House Coffee to the Postum Company, later to become part of General Foods, for $42 million. As a major stockholder, Leslie Cheek, Sr., was enriched by this sale, and soon decided to retire to enjoy travel and his interests in fishing and gardening. "My father represented the hard-won drive of his family," his son said later. He consciously emulated his father's sociability, his fastidious neatness and style in dress, and his family pride. "Both my parents were truly devoted to their life together," says the son. "They would have been happy in any case, but with children they were even happier."

The boy also admired his father's punctilious business habits, and tried to follow them. The senior Cheek was of open and sunny temperament, always courteous, and he rarely punished his children. Until he retired, he worked hard and was active in Nashville's civic and promotional affairs.

In January 1916 young Leslie entered the first grade of Peabody Demonstration School, a private school in Nashville, from which he graduated in 1926 with honors. From there he went to Duncan School, where he was an apt pupil and stood at the top of his classes. Some teachers noted that he was skilled at drawing and suggested he pursue a career in engineering or architecture. Socially he was quiet and shy, but he joined Duncan's Alpha Chi fraternity with other well-to-do boys and went to meetings each Friday night.

Though academically strong, Duncan lacked any organized athletics, so Leslie's father felt he needed "toughening." He told Mabel that Leslie ought to be sent for a summer to a military school, "to make a man out of him."

It is doubtful that Mabel would have consented to her husband's plan but for the fact that Leslie had been showing signs of adolescent moodiness that worried his mother. In her 1921 scrapbook she wrote, with uncharacteristic severity, "He has a rather peculiar disposition and is a little inclined to be very indifferent and sullen. His fond parents tried to force a smile every morning, thinking that would help him for the day, and never encouraged the temperamental part of his nature . . . Little son loved the beautiful and artistic. He was manly, honest and clean—his greatest faults being a quick temper and indifference."

Leslie was sent in 1925 to Culver Naval School in Indiana, not far from Chicago. Founded in 1894 by St. Louis industrialist Henry Culver, the school advertised that it offered, "the advantage of proper associates, a healthful moral atmosphere, personal supervising by experienced teachers, a special system of tutoring, and a beautiful and healthful location, free from the temptations and bad influences of the city, town or large watering place. Wholesome pleasures were provided in abundance, and many midshipmen affirm that their summers at Culver are the happiest they ever spent." At that time, when military preparatory schools were enjoying widespread popularity, Culver attracted about 1,000 boys.

Arriving at Culver in June 1925, young Leslie found himself without his parents or friends for the first time in his life. He was desolated by homesickness. Military life was harsh, leaving him no time to pursue his own interests. Waked for reveille at 6:30, he donned uniform, marched to breakfast, spent the morning in class and drill, and competed in sports all afternoon. After dinner, Midshipman Cheek spent most evenings in study hall, doing his homework.

Despite the jolt of his new surroundings, the youth gradually got used to Culver's rigorous life. To his surprise, he eventually liked it. Soon he was acquiring such skills as dead-reckoning and knot tying. He built himself up, joining the varsity crew and rowing a heavy ocean-going Navy cutter. In competition, Leslie's crew defeated another of older youths from Chicago's Great Lakes Naval

During the summers of 1925 through 1927, Leslie (above, center) was a midshipman at Indiana's culver Naval School. At Culver (below) he learned seamanship and self-reliance and was a member of the school's crew.

Training Station. In recognition of his leadership, he was made commander of the midshipmen corps in his final year, 1927.

He graduated from Culver with highest honors and with affection for the physical and mental discipline. As evidence, he was pleased to be invited to return in the summer of 1929 to teach navigation and signals. Still later he was to send two of his three sons there.

After the 1928 sale by the Cheek family of Maxwell House Coffee, Leslie and Mabel Cheek were able to realize their ambition to build a country estate in Nashville's Harpeth Hills, a suburban area just outside of Nashville. In 1929 they bought a hundred acres eight miles southwest of town and began to plan a large house with extensive gardens.

Mabel Cheek's family always teased her about Cheekwood's expense, but the husband and wife enjoyed building it. He liked to say it had grown out of Mabel's purchase of a ceiling-high Victorian pier mirror, which proved too big to fit the walls of the West End Avenue residence. When the mirror was stored and damaged, her husband suggested that they either sell it or build a house big enough to fit it. Mabel called his bluff, and the idea for Cheekwood was born.

Bryant Fleming, a well-known residential architect of Ithaca, New York, was selected to design the house and grounds. As the magazine *Landscape Architecture* wrote of Fleming years later:

> Practicing his belief that domestic architecture and landscape architecture must be integrated in planning from conception at the site, Mr. Fleming early in his career undertook the designing of town and country houses as well as their landscape architectural developments . . . His work also possessed an old-world charm and authenticity, obtained in part by painstaking refinement in design and the adherence to style, but also by the incorporation of genuine antiques, authentic to the period in which he was working, as architectural features or motifs.

The Cheeks first considered a Spanish design for their house and then switched to a French one. Finally they settled on a plan

In 1932, Leslie's parents completed Cheekwood, the large estate they built in the Harpeth Hills, on the outskirts of Nashville. The architect was Bryant Fleming of Ithaca, New York. The Georgian structure was placed at the top of a steep hill—three floors facing the front driveway and two looking over the Swan Lawn. (Painting: William Bailey, Lynchburg, Virginia)

LEFT: The Reflecting Pool at Cheekwood. Boxwoods and other shrubs were purchased by Cheek, Sr., an avid gardener. BELOW: The Swan Fountain was the centerpiece of the spacious lawn on the west side of Cheekwood. Leslie, Jr., designed the large doors for the loggia while an architecture student at Yale. (Courtesy, Cheekwood Botanical Gardens and Fine Arts Center, Nashville, Tennessee)

inspired by the Georgian architecture of 18th century England. They took Fleming with them on a tour of the British Isles, where they studied houses and bought decorative features and furnishings. Fleming placed the structure at the center of the tallest hill in the Cheek acreage, fitting the architecture pleasingly into the surrounding undulations. A stable and garage were nearby, discreetly hidden behind trees and shrubs.

Fleming's design incorporated a variety of woodwork and masonry features brought over from England, which were stored in a Nashville warehouse until Cheekwood was built. To match the house's large scale, furniture for the 60 rooms was bought by the Cheeks with the help of Fleming, coming chiefly from the French and Company galleries in New York and from the Duveen galleries in London. The only furniture brought from West End Avenue was Grandmother Wood's bedroom suite, which had been in the family since the 1840s.

The sloping site chosen for Cheekwood led Fleming to design a grand three-story entrance facade, with a two-story garden facade at the rear. Though Leslie was away at college and architecture school during most of Cheekwood's building, he did design the large Italianate doors for the loggia. Otherwise he played little part in the project.

When completed, Cheekwood was called "one of the last great manor houses built in the United States." One of the notable features was a Robert Adam mantel inlaid with lapis lazuli, bought in England and installed in the dining room. From Grosvenor House in London came mahogany and fruitwood doors, and from the onetime Kew Gardens palace of Queen Charlotte in London came a balustrade and spiral stairway. One 1780 chandelier used at Cheekwood was once hung in the Countess of Scarborough's house. A dome designed by Sir Christopher Wren in the 17th century was adapted by Fleming for Cheekwood's oval-shaped stair hall.

The garden was largely the creation of Leslie Cheek, senior. He bought many large

LEFT: Cheekwood, east facade, ca. 1935. **BELOW LEFT:** The living room at Cheekwood. The furnishings for the sixty-room mansion were purchased from New York's French and Company and from Duveen of London. The Warfield portraits (extreme right) measure over seven feet in height. **BELOW CENTER:** The spiral stairway in the entrance hall came from the 18th century Kew Garden palace of Britain's Queen Charlotte. **BELOW RIGHT:** The paneled library where Mabel Cheek, an insatiable reader, would sit while listening to water gently trickling through a brook in the garden beneath the window.

Mr. and Mrs. Leslie Cheek

Request the Honour of Your Presence at a

VICTORIAN STABLE PARTY

at

"CHEEKWOOD"

on the evening of July the eighteenth at nine o'clock

THE COURTESY OF A REPLY IS REQUESTED

ABOVE: Leslie's inked drawing for the invitation to Cheekwood's first large party held in the summer of 1933. The affair was held in the stable court and stalls, on the south side of the estate. At the Victorian Stable Party, guests wore costumes from the 1850s. Seated (left to right) are Leslie's grandmother Huldah Wood, father Leslie, Sr., and sister Huldah, then a student at Bryn Mawr. **ABOVE RIGHT:** In the summer of 1934 Cheekwood was the site for the B.C. Party, which derived its theme from the Periclean Age. Leslie, then an architecture student at Yale, designed the lighting, classical columns and pedestals. In the replica of a Greek temple at right, guests had their fortunes told. Serving tables were on the loggia.

boxwood he had found at old homes and farms scattered along rural roads in Virginia, Tennessee and North Carolina in the 1930s. A part-time gardener, Mr. Cheek would direct Ed Drake to halt the car whenever he spotted boxwood specimens growing near the roadway. Knocking at the door of the nearest house, he would offer to pay a generous price for the shrubbery. In the Depression years of the early 1930s, his offers to buy were rarely refused.

Bryant Fleming created a network of brooks and streams for Cheekwood's gardens, fed from a spring and recycled by pumps. The running water appealed to Mabel Cheek, who liked to read in Cheekwood's paneled library to the sound of rippling water. To pave the automobile turnaround court adjoining the house, the Cheeks bought old cobblestones from Nashville when the city repaved its streets with cement.

After they moved into Cheekwood on Thanksgiving Day 1932, the Cheeks entertained at several "dress-up" parties which were long-remembered in Nashville. At their Victorian Stable Party in 1933, they made the stables and garage into a fragment of 19th century America, where guests in costumes from Queen Victoria's day danced to jazz of the 1930s. In 1934, about 200 guests donned Greek and Roman costumes for a BC Party, elaborately staged against classical architectural settings created by Leslie Cheek, Jr.

Once he went off to college, Leslie was not to live again in Nashville for more than two or three weeks at a time. But he never lost the family ties, the sense of belonging, or the personality traits he developed at home. He would always be a southerner at heart—intuitive, romantic and mannerly. □

For his senior thesis at Yale Architecture School Cheek prepared drawings for a redesigned R.C.A. Building. The central feature of the project was this stair hall which led to a rooftop theatre-restaurant and cocktail lounge.

CHAPTER III
Harvard and Yale

Growing up in Nashville near Vanderbilt University, Leslie had always assumed he would go there to college, as did many of his local friends. One day he overheard his mother tell a friend her son was going to Harvard. He had never heard of it. His father was at first unsure that it was the right place for his son, but Mabel Cheek was insistent. "Well," Leslie's father finally conceded, "it's a very strange school, way up there in the North, and you may not like it. If you don't, son, you can come back and go to Vanderbilt." Leslie's good record at Duncan got him in with no trouble.

In the fall of 1927 Leslie Cheek boarded the train for Boston. His mother had given him written directions for reaching the Harvard Yard and notified old friends in Boston that her son was coming. But his years in Nashville and at Culver had hardly prepared the 18-year-old for the complexities of Cambridge. Many other entering students had known each other at eastern prep schools—like Choate, Groton, and Andover. A boy from Nashville would have few friends at Harvard at first.

Harvard then had nearly 3,000 undergraduates, most of them housed in dormitories around Harvard Yard. Harvard's residential houses, made possible in the 1930s by a $13 million gift from Edward S. Harkness, were only in the planning stage in 1927, and the first, Eliot House, was not ready for occupancy until 1931. Leslie was assigned to a double room in James Smith Hall, away from Harvard Yard, with a roommate whose neurotic behavior led to his commitment to a mental institution by mid-year. It was hardly an auspicious beginning for young Cheek.

Despite these difficulties, Leslie spent a busy first year making friends with the public school boys, who displayed none of the aloofness of their prep school fellows. Through his mother's connections, he received invitations to elaborate parties and entertainments held by Boston's leading families. He also attended "Friday Evenings," pre-debutante affairs held in Cambridge's Brattle Hall. He wore a full-dress suit, complete with top hat, which his father had had made for him by his Nashville tailor.

Following his father's wish, Leslie concentrated as a freshman on engineering and even contemplated post-graduate study at Harvard Business School. While the elder Cheek desired that his son pursue a business career, Leslie began to have other ideas. On his daily walk to engineering classes, he discovered the Fogg Art Museum, and realized that the fine arts—to which he had been exposed on family trips abroad—were his consuming interest. At the end of his second year he switched to a fine arts major, but the change from engineering was not easy. He would have to take additional courses over his remaining two years to make up for what he had missed. Additionally, he had to fulfill Harvard's requirements in history, language and science.

His switch to fine arts brought Leslie into contact with the faculty member who did more to shape a generation of America's art museum directors than anyone else. A member of a family that had founded Goldman Sachs investment house, Paul Sachs had gone to France after graduation from Harvard and had fallen in love with the world of art. This short, portly young man thereafter gave up a career in finance to study and collect art, eventually returning to teach at Harvard and ultimately donating his collection to its Fogg Art Museum.

The object of Sach's fine arts curriculum was to train dedicated generalists with a wide grasp of knowledge. His fierce belief in the enhancement of life through design and art appealing to all the senses yielded a wealth of curatorial talent that would distinguish Harvard for the next 50 years. Two years ahead of Leslie Cheek at Harvard was John Walker of Pittsburgh, who was to work with Andrew Mellon in the next decades to create the National Gallery of Art in Washington. Other Sachs students of the period included James Rorimer, who later headed the Metropolitan in New York; Perry Rathbone, who would direct the Boston Museum of Fine Arts; Thomas Howe, destined for San Francisco's Legion of Honor Museum; and Sherman Lee, who became director of the Cleveland Museum of Art. All of these men, and other Sachs students, would play strong supportive roles in Leslie Cheek's own museum career. They formed a network of like-minded visionaries who enhanced the place of culture in American life.

Besides Paul Sachs, young Cheek was also impressed with professor George Harold Edgell, a powerful lecturer and then head of Harvard's School of Architecture. "I believe Edgell was the most inspiring," Cheek said later. "He had charm and great knowledge." Another influence was Arthur Pope, who taught drawing and painting, and who took a keen interest in the designs which Leslie was producing for stage presentations by various Harvard clubs, including the Hasty Pudding, Pi Eta and the Dramatic clubs. Passed over by the social clubs, Cheek sought membership in those organizations which needed talent, not geneaology.

At Harvard Leslie studied perspective, life drawing and theory of drawing. Frequently for his sketching class he went by subway to the Boston Museum to spend hours copying masterpieces in detail. Feeling he needed more art instruction, Leslie spent the summer vacation after his freshman year at Peabody College in Nashville, where he further honed his skills in drawing.

His most exciting experience from his Harvard years was the summer of 1930 which he spent in West Falmouth, Massachusetts, as stage designer with the University Players. Professor Pope had been so impressed by the young man's work on Hasty Pudding and Dramatic Club plays, that he recommended Cheek for the Falmouth post. Besides Cheek and his Harvard schoolmates, Charles

REAR WALL ELEVATION for "THE MARQUISE"
U.P.G. · WEST FALMOUTH ⸺ LESLIE CHEEK JR · DESIGNER
SCALE · ½ IN.= 1 FT. ⸺ SUMMER 1930

During the summer of 1930, while an undergraduate at Harvard, Cheek worked as a guildsman with the University Players at Cape Cod. **LEFT:** Leslie's pencil drawing for a set from Noël Coward's *The Marquise* bears the research he conducted into the style of 18th century France. **ABOVE:** A photograph of the same set built following Cheek's carefully detailed plans. Note the use of lighting to create sunlight and shadow at the window at left. Later at Yale University Cheek continued to pursue his interest in theatre design.

47

THE MARQUISE

A PLAY BY NOEL COWARD

PRESENTED BY THE

UNIVERSITY PLAYERS GUILD

WEEK OF AUGUST 25th TO 30th, 1930

EVENINGS AT 8:30, WEDNESDAY MATINEE AT 2:30

TELEPHONE RESERVATIONS FALMOUTH 1250

Old Silver Beach, West Falmouth

"SUCCESS" · ACT I · THE LIBRARY (PERSPECTIVE)

Cheek designed promotional material for the University Players' production of *The Marquise,* including programs, newspaper announcements and this poster.

ABOVE: For Harvard's primitive Brattle Hall stage, Cheek drew this perspective of a library for a student play entitled *Success.* **BELOW:** The set for the library as it actually appeared. As an undergraduate, Leslie was active in Harvard's Pi Eta and Hasty Pudding clubs, and in the Cambridge School of the Drama.

In 1930 Cheek designed this set for the interior of a delapidated cabin in the Cambridge School of the Drama's presentation, *Death in the Mountains*.

Leatherbee and John Bethel, the Players' group included such future stars as Henry Fonda and Margaret Sullavan. Others were the future Broadway director Joshua Logan and actors Aleeta Freel, Myron McCormick and Kent Smith. For a brief while Cheek and Fonda were roommates.

The summer on Cape Cod drew Leslie into a talented theatrical group and deepened his interest in the theatre as a career. He designed and built sets for two of the theatre's seven productions, each of which ran for one week in July and August. On the other shows he served as a "man Friday," doing everything from painting sets to pulling the curtain rope, to dismantling shows at the end of their runs. Though small, the Playhouse was new and well-equipped. Guildsmen earned next to nothing, but they got a bed in the boys' or girls' dormitory, plus meals. More impor-

tantly, the troupe got a chance to show their skills before a sophisticated audience of vacationers—drawn mainly from Boston and New York.

They got a chance to see Cheek's handiwork at its best with *The Marquise*. For days before opening night, Cheek tirelessly worked on designs for the play's sets. He sought authenticity in settings and costumes, looking up period styles for dress and furnishings. He even sent off for a photograph of the sets for the New York premiere of this Noël Coward play, but he disregarded it when he realized it was an awkward Victorianization of a supposed 18th century French interior. With only two or three people to help him, Leslie kept busy till midnight or beyond. *The Marquise* proved a popular play, and Cheek felt rewarded.

At West Falmouth Leslie also helped

Charles Leatherbee, who owned the Playhouse, by designing posters, flyers and programs. He learned the necessity for giving each offering its own sales appeal through unique typographic design: a distinctive typeface, logotype and color scheme, with careful attention given to paper and ink selection. He also learned how to arouse public curiosity and draw larger audiences through promotion. Such showmanship would serve him in his museum career later.

At Harvard Cheek was elected to the editorial board of the school's humor magazine, *The Lampoon*, for which he designed several covers. There issued from his Westmorly Court apartment—located on Harvard's so-called "Gold Coast"—more designs for Hasty Pudding and Dramatic Club presentations. The most memorable of these was *Bulls and Belles*, for Hasty Pudding, with Spanish sets.

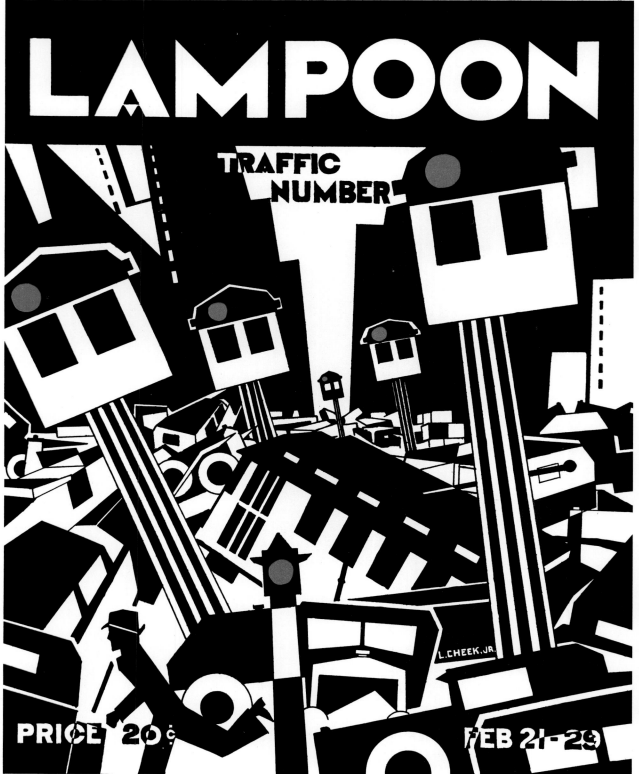

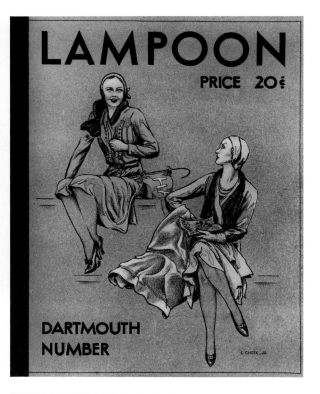

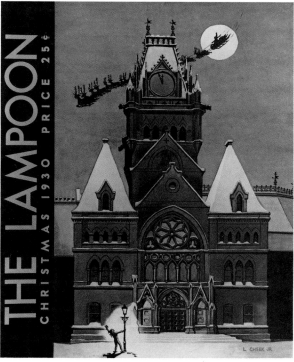

As a member of *The Lampoon* editorial board, Cheek made several cover drawings for the well-known humor magazine. His classmates were so impressed with his work that in his senior year, Leslie was asked to design the 1931 class yearbook.

Mabel Cheek journeyed from Nashville to see the spectacle. Cheek's stage directions for the play, which have survived, typify his penchant for detail, as he wrote out directions for workers erecting sets and placing spotlights.

Harvard wasn't all work, however. He went out for crew, but failed to make the varsity despite his Culver experience. Instead, he was assigned for four years to the "gentleman's crew," which rowed its shell parallel to the varsity during the lettermen's Charles River races. He and Edith "Posey" Thacher, a Radcliffe girl whom he met through his work on a dramatic production, sometimes went to the slopes of Vermont, but Leslie proved an inept skier. He often attended plays in downtown Boston and burlesque shows in Scollay Square.

When he finished in June of 1931, the young man had made a fine record. In his courses he had achieved nine A's, eight B's and five C's—good enough to secure his election to Phi Beta Kappa and the honor of graduating *magna cum laude*. His classmates chose Leslie to edit the yearbook, which was praised for its design. His parents rewarded him with a green Ford convertible. He was later to regret that his heavy concentration on the fine arts at Harvard prevented him from taking more courses in history and English literature, but at the time he found "the fine arts concentration all-absorbing." He also missed taking classes from many of the Harvard greats of his era—the philosopher Santayana, and the historians Samuel Eliot Morison and Arthur Schlesinger.

Leslie still had not settled on a career, but he knew now it would be in the arts. His father encouraged Leslie to study architecture at Yale, which accepted him for admission for September, 1931. Meanwhile, he took a summer job teaching drawing at Lake Forest Academy near Chicago. His students were embryo mid-western architects whose draftsmanship needed polishing.

Yale was to prove an even more invigorating milieu for the Tennessean than Harvard. As a graduate student, Leslie enjoyed the easy

Leslie Cheek, Sr., promised his son that if his grades at Harvard were good enough he could have as a graduation gift his choice of either a Ford or Chevrolet. Leslie, Jr., selected this Ford roadster in 1931, which he had painted dark green, a color which he thereafter continued to use for his automobiles.

While on spring vacation at Cheekwood in 1933, Leslie completed this watercolor of his grandmother Wood.

LEFT: One of Leslie Cheek's India ink *analytiques*, measuring three feet by four feet, prepared during his first year at the Yale Architecture School in 1931. **BELOW LEFT:** During his second year at Yale, Cheek was assigned *projets*, one of which called for the design of a mailbox in the lobby of an Art Deco skyscraper. **BELOW:** Another *projet* required Leslie to design the entrance to a zoo which was situated in a narrow valley. Making use of the rocky terrain, he proposed two massive tigers at the gate.

relations between students and faculty, and the school's commitment to aesthetic design as essential to man's pleasure and progress. Like his fellow-student, Eero Saarinen, Leslie Cheek soon came to see architecture as "everything from city planning to the ash tray on a living room table."

Cheek lived off-campus in New Haven in a High Street apartment, the Cambridge Arms, a short walk from the Architecture School. In four years there he had little time for socializing because of his heavy course load. "At Yale I had no buddies," he said later, "as I lived alone . . . and spent most of my time working on architectural and theatrical projects." Leslie would occasionally join fellow students in local coffee shops or snack bars. Trips to New York were fewer than among later Yalies. "New Haven had a lot of dives—joints and saloons," recalled classmate Frederick Nichols, who later became a professor of architecture at the University of Virginia. "It was really not a very nice town. There was an art movie where we saw foreign films."

Cheek spent hours in the romantic but ill-lit Weir Hall, the antique home of the Architecture School. The Gothic Revival building, near the Skull and Bones Club, was four stories tall, and first-year students began on its top floor and worked their way down in successive terms. "It was the place for many all-night sessions as students slaved over huge drawing boards to meet deadlines," Cheek remembered. It was also the scene of water battles and pranks. Sometimes students were compelled to redo time-consuming assignments which had been left unprotected during the good-natured melees. Given these hazards, Cheek preferred to complete his drawings at his apartment, and to bring them to Weir Hall for evaluation.

The most talented member of Cheek's class, which numbered about 100, was Eero Saarinen, son of Finnish-born modernist architect Eliel Saarinen, who had come to the United States with his family in 1923 and developed Cranbrook Academy of Art near Detroit. The younger Saarinen, who was older than his Yale classmates and had studied sculpture in Paris, soon advanced to second-year work and graduated ahead of his starting class. Cheek recalled that Eero's work was always so much more advanced in concept and execution than anyone else's, including that of the professors.

Portly Everett Meeks was dean of the Yale School of Fine Arts, and his imprint was strong. Leslie, who took Meeks' comprehensive course in architectural history, remembered the dean as a kind and humorous man whose door was always open to students.

Meeks was an adherent of the 19th century Beaux Arts tradition of architectural training—a totalist approach, which called for instruction in painting, sculpture and architecture. Professionals, mostly from New York, came to Yale to judge students' work. Among these visitors was Raymond Hood, designer of New York's RCA and American Radiator buildings, and industrial designer Norman Bel Geddes, who offered Cheek a job.

Teams of Yale students would be assigned problems by the New York Beaux Arts Institute. Entries would be judged by practicing architects in competition with entries submitted by other schools. The high point of each term came when students submitted designs for the annual Beaux Arts scholarships to Paris, and the Prix de Rome awards for study in Italy.

During the Meeks regime, Yale won the lion's share of prizes for these international competitions. Indeed, wrote one critic, "Under his guidance, New Haven's genteel art academy . . . developed into one of the foremost professional training grounds in the country." But Meeks modified the traditionalist approach with modernist influences. By bringing in critics like Wallace Harrison who were noted for their contemporary designs, Meeks saw to it that his students' classical training was made relevant to the times. Leslie Cheek's taste was to reflect the blend Everett Meeks sought—a taste rooted in the traditional yet clearly influenced by modernism.

As a first year student, Cheek spent much of his time drawing designs to solve architectural problems assigned by the Beaux Arts Institute. The 3 by 4 foot India ink drawings were called *analytiques*. A typical *analytique* called for a loggia to be added to an already existing classical structure, presumably in Rome or Paris. Cheek won a "first mention" for his design for an American embassy building.

In his second year, Cheek's class was given harder problems, called *projets*. Third and fourth year assignments were still more difficult, requiring collaborative efforts between several students to deal with the architectural, painting and sculptural needs of a particular design.

During his third year, Cheek and two fine arts classmates submitted an entry in the Prix de Rome competition, sponsored by the Association of the Alumni of the American Academy in Rome. The problem called for a redesign of New York's famed Times Square. Leonard Haber, a painting student, and Raymond G. Barger, a sculpture student, joined Cheek in developing the called-for design and model. The *New York Times* of January 20, 1934, announced that three teams had tied for first place, including the Cheek-Haber-Barger group, plus one other from Yale.

However, Cheek's biggest undertaking was his fourth-year thesis: a re-design of the top ten floors of an 85-story skyscraper. Cheek chose to improve the upper floors of the recently finished RCA Building, a bold choice, since his critic was to be Raymond Hood (1881–1934), whose firm had originally designed this modern skyscraper.

Cheek spent many hours designing a greatly enlarged Rainbow Room to occupy the building's top two floors. The central feature of this scheme was a huge oval-shaped theatre-restaurant, with a revolving stage, divided into halves, one on a hydraulic lift. While one half of the stage was being viewed by the audience, the other half was being lowered to a service area on the floor below where sets could be changed. The stage was surrounded on three sides by eight tiered dining levels, rising in

Leonard Haber's rendering of a redesigned Times Square for the 1934 Prix de Rome collaborative competition. The entry submitted by Haber, Leslie Cheek and Raymond Barger tied for first place in the judging. At the base of the skyscraper (center left) is an illuminated stepped fountain, Cheek's principal contribution to the team's submission. (Courtesy, Leonard Haber)

For his senior thesis at Yale, Leslie proposed to redesign the top ten floors of the recently completed R.C.A. Building in Manhattan. Cheek's ambitious plan called for a roof-top theatre-restaurant with adjoining cocktail lounge, both affording dramatic views of the city below. On the roof itself was to be a garden with observation platform. This rendering by John Wenrich shows how the building's original architect, Raymond Hood, envisioned the completed skyscraper. (Photo courtesy of Rockefeller Center Management Corporation, New York)

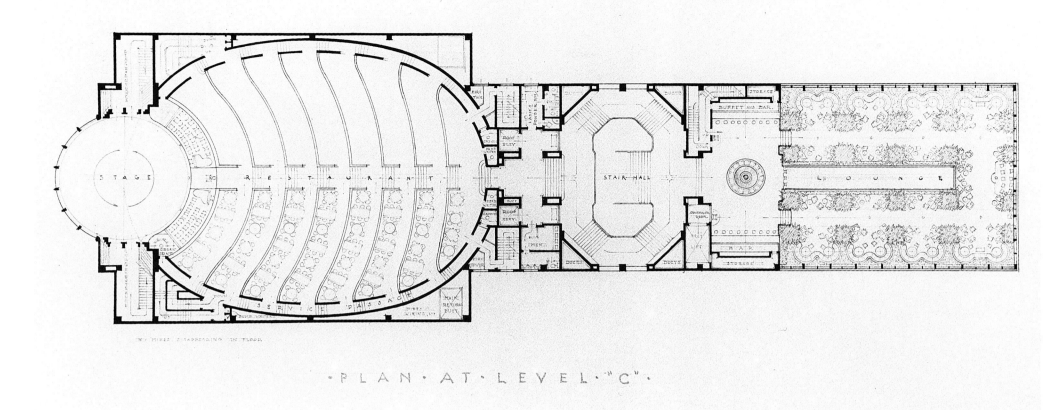

·P·L·A·N·AT·L·E·V·E·L·"C"·

This section shows the cocktail lounge (right) and dinner theatre (left) separated by the stair hall. The lounge had plantings of trees and shrubbery, cultivated in a special roof-top greenhouse, plus a trickling fountain. In the dinner theatre, the revolving circular stage was surrounded by eight tiered dining levels, and could be lowered or raised by an hydraulic lift for scene changes. Cheek designed serving passages at either side of the dining levels so that waiters moving about would not interrupt the diners' enjoyment of the performances.

concentric circles. From their tables, diners would have unobstructed views through the tremendous plate glass windows behind the stage to downtown Manhattan and the East and Hudson rivers.

Connecting the theatre restaurant with a magnificent "greenhouse" cocktail lounge, was an impressive entrance hall, dominated by a graceful stairway and a huge chandelier. Luxurious burnt-orange velvet covered the walls, with a carpet of deeper hue. In Art Deco manner, narrow chrome strips defined the corners and edges of the hall, and chrome was repeated in the stairway railing, with insets of ornamental beveled stars in clear glass.

The cocktail lounge had a glass roof high enough to permit large trees and shrubs to grow in tubs between booths and tables. In the center a pool was fed from a fountain at the higher entrance level, where two bars were located. Greenery for this room was supplied by a rooftop nursery reached by a service elevator.

Guests were to pause in the lounge to enjoy a pre-show drink. An elaborate fountain—really a giant sun-dial whose central figure was in the form of a female nude—kept track of the minutes remaining until showtime. The sculpture's finger cast a shadow on the face of the carved dial indicating the exact hour. At showtime, patrons proceeded by the

stairway up to the restaurant entrance, where a maître d' had them shown to their seats. At each show's conclusion, the stage was lowered, its sets were removed, and it was raised again to form a dance floor with a view of all of the city below.

Raymond Hood died in 1934, thus none of the senior student's proposed improvements were made to the original design. The Rainbow Room remains today much as Hood planned it.

The mathematics Leslie had taken at Harvard exempted him from engineering at Yale and gave him an opportunity to devote time to theatre studies. Cheek was to be greatly influenced by Donald Oenslager, of

Though Cheek was an architecture student, problems in theatre design still fascinated him. He enrolled in several Yale Drama School courses, including one taught by stage designer Donald Oenslager. One of the assignments was for Leslie to create settings for the three-act mystical play *The Sunken Bell* by German playwright Gerhardt Hauptmann.

RIGHT: Donald Oenslager, the young professor of stage design at Yale, would have a lasting influence on Cheek. For Oenslager's course, Leslie completed set designs for Verdi's opera *Aida.* Having visited Egypt in 1927 with his parents, he knew how to re-create the mysterious land of the pharoahs. **FAR RIGHT:** The voluptuous nudes Cheek depicted in the "Apartment of Amneris" attracted the attention of New Yorker Earl Carroll, who offered him a job with his *Vanities,* but the young student declined at his mother's and Oenslager's urging.

Broadway fame, "a magnificent teacher" of stage design. Oenslager, who was to become a life-long friend, would lecture on a period of stage design, have students read a play from the era, and then have them design sets for it. His heavy demands kept Cheek working late into nights on such works as *Julius Caesar, The Sunken Bell, A Month in the Country* and *Children of Darkness*. Cheek's designs for *Aïda* were placed on display and seen by New York showman Earl Carroll, who produced *Earl Carroll's Vanities*, glorifying beautiful show girls. Carroll sought out the young man who had rendered such voluptuous nudes in his Egyptian scenery designs and offered Cheek a job, but Mabel Cheek and Oenslager persuaded Leslie not to accept.

Stanley McCandless, who offered a course in stage lighting, was also influential. In his museum career later, Cheek clearly followed McCandless' dictum that light "should be thought of as a new material to serve definite functions . . . It is a plastic medium which fills space very much like clay or brick or stone . . . Lighting can be designed so that it gives not only visibility but comfort, composition to things seen, and to some extent atmosphere."

When a play by Cheek's fellow student Edward Reveaux, titled *Names in Bronze* was chosen by the faculty for production in April of 1934, Oenslager chose Cheek to design sets for acts one and three, with fellow student Sam Leve assigned act two. It was a weak play, but it gave Leslie an opportunity to work intently on a serious stage project which would actually be performed by Yale School of Drama students.

Leonard Haber thought his Tennessean classmate "had a lot of charm." Recalling Cheek's Yale years, he said, "He knew the value of public relations and how to exercise it." He also had humor, independence and self-confidence. Undoubtedly, his $200 monthly allowance, comfortable apartment, and green Ford set him apart from most hard-pressed fine arts students. "He was an achiever," Haber recalls, "but he didn't always

RIGHT: As a first year student at the Yale Architecture School, Cheek was required to take a life drawing class. While he was sketching this amateur model, the girl's angry mother suddenly burst into the studio and forced her to dress and leave.

57

In 1934 the Drama School faculty chose Cheek to design scenery for two of the three acts of Edward Reveaux's *Names in Bronze*. It gave Leslie a rare opportunity at Yale to create sets which would be used in an actual production. **ABOVE:** His watercolor for Act II, "The Apartment in New York." **BELOW:** A photo of the same set.

Cheek was always fond of costume parties, and in 1935 he went as a Scotsman to the Yale Beaux Arts Ball. With him is Edith "Posey" Thacher, a Radcliffe graduate whom he dated for several years.

For the 1935 Beaux Arts Ball, Cheek converted the lecture hall at Yale's Art Gallery into a Medieval Hall, complete with imitation stained glass windows made of paper, and soaring arches cut out of black cloth.

make allowances for other people's shortcomings."

As Leslie's graduation approached in 1935, he was chosen to create, with the aid of other classmates, a medieval setting for the biennial Beaux Arts Ball held by the fine arts students in the old Yale Art Gallery. Adhering to Leslie's plan, they transformed the lecture hall into a medieval abbey through the use of cut-out arches, made of black cloth trimmed with gold edging. Plump Dean Meeks as "God the Father" beamed down from an imitation stained glass window at one end of the hall. He was portrayed as a medieval abbot, with one of his big toes poking indecorously out of a white athletic sock.

At the stroke of midnight students dressed as knights, monks, courtesans, princesses and jesters formed a procession for the grand march. At the end rode "Lady Godiva," recognizable beneath a seductive semi-nudity and ample bosom as a male student, Taylor Simmons. Godiva's spirited horse was an amalgam of two other students, the head and front legs being Freddie Nichols. Vincent Price, at that time a Yale University senior and later the star of horror films, came dressed as a peasant. "Everyone cooperated in the undertaking," Leslie said happily when the work was over.

Despite his fascination with the theatre, Leslie was determined to become an architect. After he graduated from Yale in June 1935, he went to New York to call on Chester Aldrich, a partner in the well-known architectural firm of Delano and Aldrich. He was kindly received, but Aldrich led him to the firm's drafting room and showed Leslie draftsmen seated before empty drawing boards with nothing to do. The Depression had put a halt to virtually all building.

The would-be architect packed up his belongings and went home to Nashville. The future seemed cloudy indeed. ☐

Leslie Cheek's watercolor of the St. George Tucker House, painted in Williamsburg during the summer of 1935. Cheek was then touring the South preparing a portfolio of architectural renderings and sketches.

CHAPTER IV

The Williamsburg Years

ABOVE: William and Mary president John Stewart Bryan was an enthusiastic supporter of Leslie's plans for a fine arts department, which brought to reality Thomas Jefferson's dream of 1779 (Photo: Thomas L. Williams, Williamsburg, Virginia). **LEFT:** While painting watercolors in Colonial Williamsburg, including this of the restored Capitol, Cheek met Curator James Cogar, who introduced Cheek to president Bryan.

Discouraged to find no openings for an architect when he left Yale, Leslie Cheek drove his green Ford loaded with his possessions home to Nashville. At 26 he had faced the first major disappointment of his life. Though he had graduated with honors, he discovered that the Depression had halted construction all over the nation. Nobody needed an architect.

As usual, Leslie found his parents understanding. His father offered to help his son do whatever he wished. Leslie's decision was to travel through the South painting watercolors that he could submit to an architectural firm—perhaps in Nashville—to land him a job. He already had a start, for he and Fred Nichols had gone to Charleston before graduating to make sketches for Dean Meeks' Yale architectural history course.

Starting in Nashville, where he began by sketching Grandmother Wood and Cheekwood's formal gardens, he moved on to Baltimore, then Annapolis. From there, he motored to Williamsburg where, despite the Depression, scholars and artisans were at work restoring Virginia's 18th century capital. The restoration project, which had been announced in 1928, was underwritten by John D. Rockefeller, Jr.

One morning in the Summer of 1935 Cheek set up his folding stool outside the newly rebuilt Williamsburg Capitol of 1704, and began to draw under an ancient mulberry tree on Duke of Gloucester Street. Behind him were the houses and taverns of Williamsburg's main thoroughfare, reaching to the College of William and Mary, chartered in 1693, at the far end of the street nearly a mile away. Among the passers-by who paused to observe Cheek at work was James L. Cogar, a former student at the Yale School of Fine Arts, who was the youthful curator of Colonial Williamsburg.

The two fell into conversation. "He had just graduated from Yale, and I had had to stop studying architecture there because of illness, so we had an interesting talk," Cogar recalled. They became friends, and later Cogar went to the college's president, John Stewart Bryan, and recommended that Cheek be appointed to teach Cogar's 18th century social history course while the curator travelled to England for Colonial Williamsburg during one college semester.

The worldly Bryan, publisher of the *Richmond News Leader* and an overseer of Harvard, had been inaugurated president only a year before. The tall, aristocratic Richmonder had immediately set out to strengthen the state-supported college's liberal arts offerings, to improve the quality and pay of the faculty, and to lift the school's morale which was affected by the hard times.

Bryan was instantly drawn to the confident, determined Leslie Cheek. They shared similar backgrounds of wealth, travel and interest in the arts. Bryan hired the Tennessean to take over for Cogar, and Cheek flung himself into finding and making slides for his illustrated lectures. He took photographs of hundreds of historic buildings, developing them himself alone at night in the college's chemistry department lab. When school opened, he projected them for his classes— the first lectures given at William and Mary to utilize such slides.

The success of Cheek's courses suggested to him that the college should include them in a full-fledged Department of Fine Arts. Already the college had training in theatre, directed by Althea Hunt, and also offered courses in musical history taught by George Small. Several American colleges, influenced by the pioneering work at Harvard and Yale, had introduced undergraduate fine arts courses. Only a few colleges in the South had done so by 1935. Cheek proposed to offer the history of painting, sculpture and architecture primarily as cultural background for liberal arts students, but also as preparation for post-graduate concentration in these fields.

Cheek's proposals met with President Bryan's enthusiasm. In 1779, Governor Thomas Jefferson had during the Revolution unsuccessfully tried to introduce the arts into William and Mary's curriculum. Now, 160 years later, Jefferson's dream was to be realized. Bryan offered Cheek space for the new department in the Taliaferro Building, an unused dormitory. He also authorized Cheek to enlist teachers of painting and sculpture and directed bursar Charles E. Duke to provide the money to carry out Cheek's designs for the Taliaferro Building's conversion into classrooms.

Cheek recommended two Yale colleagues for the fine arts professorships: Edwin C. Rust, a young sculptor from Memphis, and Leonard Haber, a painter from New York, with whom Cheek had worked on Beaux Arts competitions. President Bryan met Haber in New York for his first interview at the University Club on Fifth Avenue. The mannered Bryan impressed the young painter as "a Van Dyck type of man," and he urged Haber to come to Williamsburg to see if he liked it. Haber did and accepted the job, as did Rust.

To create space for teaching the fine arts, the interior of the Taliferro Building was radically altered. "We gutted it, tore off the two porches, and created our own lecture room, library and even a simple air-conditioning system," Cheek recalls. Air-conditioning, hitherto rare in America, was introduced primarily to eliminate heat in the windowless black slide projection room, which had a stepped floor to which were bolted 60 seats. Exhaust fans were installed in the attic, which sucked air through double-louvers inserted in the window frames. It was the first air-conditioning in Williamsburg. Other firsts soon came thick and fast.

In the remodelled Taliaferro Building, the first floor was devoted to sculpture and the construction of stage sets; the second to architecture, the lecture room, library and faculty dining room; and the third to painting and drawing. These rooms were reached via a

three-story open stairwell, the center of which was dominated by a wall fountain, with a mirrored pool and goldfish at its base. Rust created a lighted bas-relief wall-sculpture of nymphs and undersea life, which was covered by large sheets of plate glass, over which water trickled to the pool below. The effect was highly dramatic.

The departmental library had three long, built-in reading tables, at the ends of which were plant boxes and windows. Facing these was the librarians' curved desk, behind which were bookcases the length of the wall. Many of the volumes were given by the Carnegie Foundation for the Advancement of Teaching. This room was painted light green, with gray carpeting, and furnishings were of blond wood. Adjoining the library was the lecture room where slides of art works were reflected on the wall screen. Because so few color photographic views were then available, Professors Cheek, Haber and Rust spent their summer vacations clipping color prints for their courses from books and magazines.

There was the high-ceilinged workroom on the first floor for constructing scenery for college plays, and a small dining room on the second floor where the staff lunched. Haber later remarked that this lunchroom's placement in the Taliaferro Building had given morale and cohesion to the new department, since faculty could dine together and discuss problems and plans. President Bryan often attended these informal luncheon conferences, along with other guests, including students.

The Fine Arts Department stood out as an oasis of contemporary elegance against the backdrop of the old college, much of which was still in the grip of the Depression. In the Williamsburg of Cheek's years, little more than the Wren Building had yet been restored utilizing Rockefeller funds between 1928 and 1932. But Cheek saw the possibilities of the town's restoration, which was to cost over $65 million.

President Bryan dedicated the Fine Arts building in February of 1937. Mabel Cheek

ABOVE: The Fine Arts Department was housed in a remodelled dormitory—the Taliaferro Building. Included was this second floor library. The specially-made furnishings had maple tops and grey-green leather coverings, which matched the hue of the carpet. Walls were light grey; the ceiling, white; the columns and trim, silver-gold. The design included indirect lighting for shadowless reading.
RIGHT: Sculpture, taught by Edwin C. Rust, was one of the courses offered by the new Fine Arts Department. This studio was on the first floor of the renovated Taliaferro Building.

came from Nashville and Huldah from Bryn Mawr. But Leslie Cheek Senior had died of a heart attack in October 1935, just as his son was embarking on his career. Calling on his promotional experience from his summer theatre days at West Falmouth, Cheek arranged a series of social events for the dedication ceremonies which attracted art critics and patrons from Richmond, Washington, Norfolk and Nashville, along with the college's friends, students and alumni.

Students found Cheek's instruction fascinating but difficult. Wrote John Jennings, one of Cheek's first architectural history students who was later to be director of the Virginia Historical Society, "I was warned by all of your credit-seeking students you were the toughest, most demanding 'grader' at college." Jennings agreed, but was glad he had audited Cheek's class.

The department's innovative courses attracted wide attention. *Art News Magazine* devoted an article to the "Southern Renaissance," while the *Magazine of Art* carried a six-page illustrated article by Cheek. It bore the subtitle, "A New Kind of College Art Department."

Cheek found the best opportunity for faculty and student collaboration in the student plays which Althea Hunt produced six times yearly. Having designed sets and costumes at Harvard and Yale, Leslie took over similar duties for the college's theatre. He called on the talents of Haber and Rust, and, of course, on students, who built elaborate sets. Writing of this period in *The William and Mary Theatre*, edited by Althea Hunt and published in 1965, student-actor Carl Buffington, of the 1938 class, wrote:

The establishment of a department of fine arts at the College of William and Mary filled a long-felt need in Williamsburg. In addition to the plays—one of the few diversions the little Restoration College town had to offer—townspeople, faculty, and students now could anticipate art exhibits ranging from borrowed collections from New York's Museum of Modern Art to original drawings by top

RIGHT: Cheek lived in this small restored kitchen located at the corner of Palace Green and Duke of Gloucester Street, near Bruton Parish Church. BELOW: His Art Deco interior raised eyebrows. The only source of heat was the fireplace. The two couches converted to guest beds, though there was a tiny bedroom and bath. Note the indirect lighting installed in the top of the mantle.

The memorable railroad embankment scene from the College's production of Ferenc Molnar's *Liliom*. This set and others reflected Cheek's training at Yale in the latest stage design and lighting techniques.

contemporary set designers in the American theatre . . . From the moment he arrived in Williamsburg, Leslie Cheek exerted a considerable influence on the William and Mary theatre . . . The . . . theatre, which had operated autonomously for many years, now became a part of the new Department of Fine Arts. One of Mr. Cheek's first goals was to make the William and Mary theatre one of the best college theatres in the country. No one doubted his ability to do it.

He was a superb designer. He was a perfectionist . . . He was a man of enormous drive . . . a relentless taskmaster to his crews, yet completely devoted to them, as they were to him. The results of his labors were sometimes superlative.

The plays were performed in Phi Beta Kappa Hall, which had a small stage but lacked a sloping floor. Especially memorable was the performance of Alberto Caselli's romantic melodrama, *Death Takes a Holiday*, for which Leslie designed sets, furniture and costumes. The theatre also won praise for its staging of Gilbert and Sullivan operas and of Ferenc Molnar's *Liliom*. Said Carl Buffington, "[Cheek's] railroad embankment set for *Liliom* deserves a place in any collection of great stage sets. I have never seen a better one."

"Leslie Cheek improved William and Mary's plays because of his training under Donald Oenslager at Yale," Leonard Haber said later. In their years at the college, Cheek usually invited a Yale designer to come to Williamsburg to execute the costumes for a show. "We did sets comparable to those they did on Broadway," Haber recalls. Professor Edwin Rust recalled *Liliom*. "At Les' suggestion, our great and good friend, Charles Harrison, in the English department, and I did continuous musical background, complete with leitmotifs. This was made possible by the recently-acquired Carnegie gift of recordings." Rust later became director of the Memphis School of Fine Art, while Harrison became dean of the University of the South at Sewanee, Tennessee.

To the small but lively college, Cheek brought leaders in American art, including

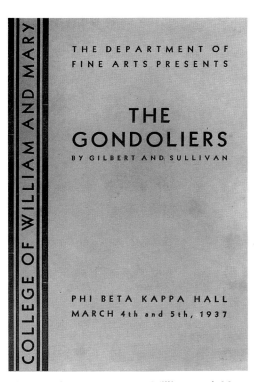

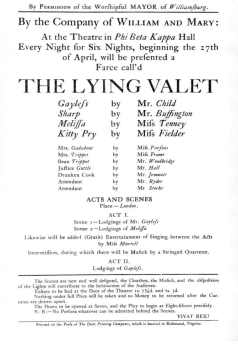

ABOVE: Two layouts for programs to William and Mary productions exemplify Cheek's desire to make the typographic styles reflect the character of the stage presentations: the stylized contemporary sophistication of an updated Gilbert and Sullivan musical contrasts with the 18th century hand-set type for *The Lying Valet*. BELOW: The stage set from *The Gondoliers*. The Fine Arts Department annually invited a Yale faculty member to design costumes for a College production.

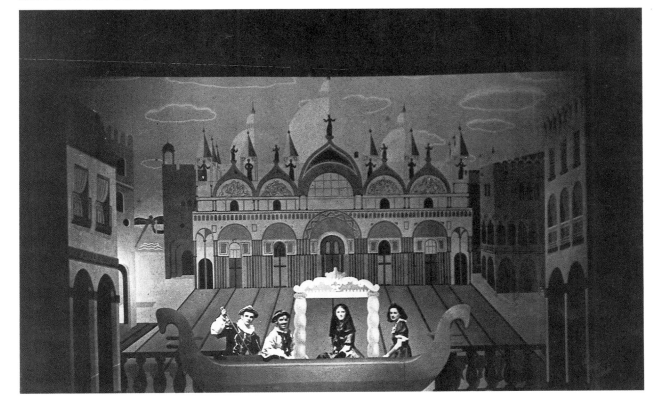

Frank Lloyd Wright and Georgia O'Keeffe. Wright came to Williamsburg in 1938 to speak at the preview of an exhibition Cheek had borrowed from the Museum of Modern Art in New York. It was the first Wright show ever staged in the South, and the unconventional designer made national headlines by criticizing the architecture of Williamsburg as being unsuited to Virginia's weather. Next morning, after a breakfast of Smithfield ham and spoonbread with Bryan at the President's House, he wrote in the guest book, "Frank Lloyd Wright and wife Algivanne, after a breakfast that justifies 'The Restoration.'"

Cheek also invited the famous American painter Georgia O'Keeffe to attend the opening of the college's exhibition of her works. Though she had spent a decade of her life in Williamsburg in the early 1900s, she had not been back to town for 30 years. Shy and taciturn, the artist declined to make a speech after President Bryan presented her honorary degree. "She seemed to be in some other world," said Cheek, who shepherded the tall, severe artist through the day's events. Later, Abby Aldrich Rockefeller presented the college with one of Miss O'Keeffe's paintings.

One of Leslie Cheek's most challenging assignments at the college was to produce President Bryan's annual Christmas Party and June Ball, both made possible largely through Bryan's generosity. In those Depression years, Williamsburg and the college remained poor and austere. To add pleasure to their lives, Cheek recalls, "Mr. Bryan felt students should go home in December and June with happy memories." Those who attended them never forgot the beauty and originality of these extravaganzas.

Cheek chose landscape architect Charles Gillette's newly-created Sunken Garden on the campus behind the Wren Building as the setting for the June Ball. Leslie laid a dance floor with elaborate garden decorations and lighting, and erected chaperons' boxes in front of the boxwood lining the area.

Even more ornate were the Christmas parties. In the 1930s, William and Mary oper-

ABOVE: Frank Lloyd Wright (left) with Leslie Cheek at the William and Mary exhibition of the architect's work, which opened in 1938. **LEFT:** The exhibition, designed by Cheek, was in Phi Beta Kappa Hall, and attracted the attention of Henry Treide, then president of the Baltimore Museum of Art, who later offered Cheek the director's post there.

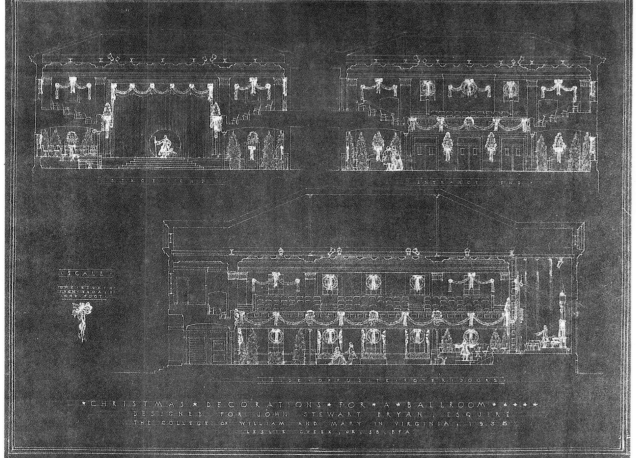

William and Mary president John Stewart Bryan, the "Lord of the Revels" (right), escorts Mrs. Douglas Southall Freeman to the dais at the Christmas Ball. Behind them are Williamsburg's Mayor and Mrs. Channing Hall.

Prepared at president Bryan's request, these are Cheek's detailed plans for the 1935 Christmas Ball, complete with places for green garlands, red bows and lighted candles.

68

ated on a two-semester term, and students would leave for Christmas holiday dreading the examinations they faced when they returned after the New Year. Bryan and Cheek wanted to give the departing students a memorable send-off, one which would erase any anxieties about the approaching examinations. Accordingly, they devised the Christmas Party to bring together in one joyous occasion all of the college's 1,200 students and 100 faculty and staff. For the occasion, Cheek and his assistants turned Phi Beta Kappa Hall into a Georgian-style "Great Hall," with miles of laurel garlands, a profusion of holly wreaths, lighted candles and red ribbons.

The party's climax came when the tall, bespectacled Bryan ascended the forestage. Dressed as "Lord of the Revels" in full-bottomed wig and colonial breeches, he presided over the evening's performance. Around him stood a court of senior faculty and staff members with their wives. A costumed "Lord of Misrule"—usually professor of physical education Tucker Jones—bellowed introductions as Bryan's guests entered with their escorts and took seats onstage. Among the guests were Douglas Southall Freeman and his wife, of Richmond, he being editor of Bryan's *Richmond News Leader* and a popular lecturer at the college on current affairs. They were introduced by the Lord of Misrule as "Sir Douglas and Lady Freeman, of Westbourne," a reference to their Richmond home.

After such Christmas festivities as bringing in the yule log and the singing of carols, fraternity and sorority members, dressed in rented or borrowed costumes, would perform skits. When one of these dealt with Greek mythology, Dean Grace Warren Landrum complained about some of the coeds' very revealing dresses. President Bryan later asked Cheek if he had supervised costumes. "Dean Landrum thought the goddesses were too Greek," Cheek chuckled later.

At midnight, refreshments were served at buffet tables in the Dodge Room of Phi Beta Kappa Hall, after which guests danced to music by Hal Kemp's popular orchestra. Cheek

Students and faculty gather as president Bryan presides at the Christmas Ball. The "Lord of Misrule" is announcing that the undergraduates are about to perform their skits. Note the huge coat of arms with lion and unicorn, which was made in England.

Cheek had Spanish moss sent from South Carolina for the 1938 "Homecoming Ball," held at the College's Blow Gymnasium. Scenery "columns," window shutters and railings created a Greek Revival scene.

A Vassar yearbook photograph of Mary Tyler Freeman. After graduating from college in 1937, Mary Tyler considered becoming a journalist like her father, Douglas Southall Freeman, the Pulitzer-prize-winning biographer of George Washington and Robert E. Lee.

had decorated the serving tables with cornucopias, covered in golden foil and filled with fruit, with serving men in English livery.

Another affair which Williamsburg long remembered was the Fine Arts Department's 1938 Surrealist Ball, held in the Wren Building's spacious cellar. Each of the building's English cellar window recesses held a surrealist scene, eerily lighted. President Bryan showed up in academic gown, dragging a wheeled toy which squawked. Professor Leonard Haber pasted the two ends of an arrow against his head to look as if his skull had been pierced.

In the College Yard in front of the Wren Building, Cheek tethered a white cow, bathed in purple light. It illustrated Edward Lear's nonsense verse, "I Never Saw a Purple Cow." One guest, A. Edwin Kendrew, director of Colonial Williamsburg's architecture department, tried to milk the beast, for which Cheek was later billed for one quart by the animal's owner.

During his years as Chairman of the Fine Arts Department, Leslie Cheek lived in a small restored Colonial Williamsburg kitchen building, in which he installed an Art Deco interior. When a restoration official questioned the appropriateness of Cheek's decor, Abby Aldrich Rockefeller came to the young man's defense, pronouncing it "thoroughly charming," and declaring she "wouldn't think of changing it." In his bachelor quarters Cheek entertained friends and students alike. Among them were Richard Velz, who later worked under Cheek at the Virginia Museum, Marian Hinman, later Mrs. Martin Gracey, and Mae Wright, later Mrs. Joseph Reid.

In 1937, when Leslie Cheek was 29, he met Mary Tyler Freeman. She was the daughter of Douglas Southall and Inez Goddin Freeman. Occasionally Mary Tyler accompanied her father to Williamsburg for his lectures at the college, and on one of these visits Cheek invited the Freemans to join him for lunch at the Fine Arts Department building. Mary Tyler had heard about Leslie Cheek from her father's friend, John Stewart Bryan, and was anxious to meet him. Leslie had also heard about the slender girl.

The two shared many interests and friends. Mary Tyler was 20, a recent graduate of Vassar, and intended to be a journalist and writer like her father, the biographer of George Washington and Robert E. Lee. When she met Cheek, she was considering entering the graduate school of journalism at Columbia University. But she was instantly intrigued by Leslie, who was similarly enchanted by her. Soon after she met Cheek, Mary Tyler and her father were injured in an automobile accident in North Carolina. While she recovered, Leslie visited her sickroom in Richmond and asked her to become secretary and librarian at the Fine Arts Department for the term beginning the following September. She accepted, and that fall moved to Williamsburg to share quarters in the restored kitchen building of the Travis House with Cora Tomlinson, president Bryan's secretary.

On October 28, 1938—his 30th birthday—Leslie Cheek asked Mary Tyler Freeman to marry him. She happily consented, and the two agreed to keep their engagement a secret from all but their families.

When news of their engagement was announced in February of 1939, friends recognized it as a inspired choice for both Leslie and Mary Tyler. He was a highly intuitive, artistic man, able to conceive and carry out a wealth of creative undertakings. His fiancée had her mother's tact and grace, her father's talents for organization and observation, and some of his literary gifts. As the eldest of three children, she had a strong sense of family responsibility. Above all, she had a lively sense of humor and enjoyed the arts, travel and good living, as Leslie did.

Once they became engaged, Mary Tyler felt obliged to resign her job in the department, and to return to Richmond in March 1938. "Mother didn't want all the girls at William and Mary to think they could marry their professors," she said.

While Mary Tyler made plans for a June wedding, Leslie was confronting another deci-

In 1938-39 the American National Theatre and Academy sponsored a competition for a Williamsburg festival theatre and fine arts center. Here the jury (Cheek is at right) examines Eero Saarinen's winning design.

sion: whether or not to become director of the Baltimore Museum of Art. The museum's president, Henry Treide, had visited William and Mary where he had been impressed with Cheek's Frank Lloyd Wright exhibition. Several months later, when he encounted Cheek at a party in Baltimore, he asked the young man if he would like to head that city's art museum, soon to celebrate its 25th anniversary, and then in search of a director.

It was a difficult decision for Leslie. The fine arts were beginning to make an impact at William and Mary. "The department made a great contribution," says Leonard Haber.

"The instructors from Yale were tops. They gave William and Mary as good a department as in any undergraduate school. And Leslie's foresight did it, with the full support of Mr. Bryan." Ted Rust, who would eventually succeed Cheek as departmental chairman, credited the department's success to the faculty's "relaxed, informal, first-name-basis relationship with a wonderful group of dedicated, talented and hard-working students."

But given the college's limited size and funds, how much further could the "renaissance" go? Leslie interpreted the Baltimore offer as an augury that he should move along.

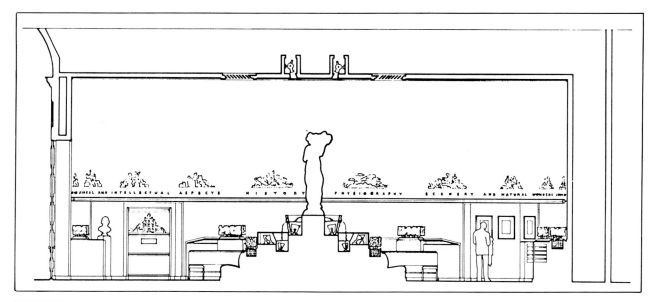

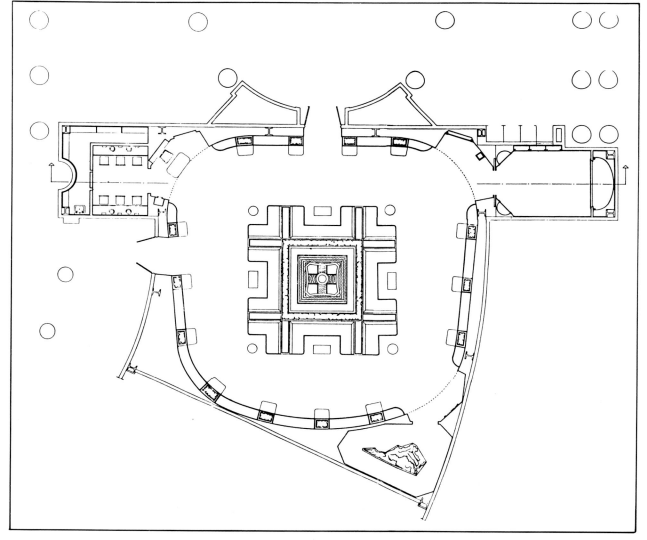

LEFT: Leslie Cheek's drawing for the "Virginia Room" at the 1939 New York World's Fair. The sculpture at the room's center was dramatically lit by spotlights above the ceiling and in its base. **BELOW LEFT:** The plan of the "Virginia Room." Its unusual shape was dictated by the pavilion in which it was located. Along the walls were illustrated albums with views of the state's history, natural beauty and resources. Visitors used the room at the top left for writing picture postcards. A pantry was in the room at upper right. A large three-dimensional relief map of the state was in the gallery at lower right. **BELOW:** Weary tourists examine albums beneath Edwin Rust's soaring contemporary sculpture honoring Virginia's rivers. Cheek's design for this space won praise for its elegance and comfort.

"I think he was waiting to see where life guided him," Mary Tyler remembers. "He was very happy in Williamsburg. He loved it. But I think he would have found it stifling—so orderly and without the action and excitement of a city. Baltimore was a much larger opportunity for him."

The truth was that Leslie still wished to become an architect and he believed that the Baltimore Museum directorship might lead to it. His interest in building design was at that time stirred anew by a competition for a William and Mary college theatre. In 1938, Cheek had persuaded A. Conger Goodyear, president of New York's Museum of Modern Art and also head of the newly-formed American National Theatre and Academy (ANTA) to consider locating the National Festival Theatre in Williamsburg.

The competition for the building design, sponsored by ANTA, was held in 1938-39, with Williamsburg selected as the site because America's first theatre had been built there in the early 1700s. Further, it was hoped that the Rockefeller interests would contribute to the project. Over 120 designs were submitted by such architects as Walter Gropius, Wallace Harrison, Richard Neutra and Marcel Breuer. Cheek was selected to be a judge, along with five other men, among them *House Beautiful* editor Kenneth Stowell.

The winning entry was submitted by a design team headed by Leslie's Yale schoolmate, Eero Saarinen. However, Leslie could offer little help to ANTA's ambitious hope to build the Williamsburg complex, which was estimated to cost $995,000, excluding the cost of the site. He knew that William and Mary was hard pressed to meet its existing budgets, for the Depression still held America in its grip.

Besides, the clouds of war were gathering, and the college and Williamsburg's restorers faced new problems. The Saarinen-designed building was never constructed in Williamsburg. Instead, in 1957 William and Mary was to get a fine new 750-seat theatre after the original Phi Beta Kappa Hall burned in 1954. In 1968 a new Andrews Fine Arts Building was attached to the 1957 Phi Beta Kappa Hall, enabling the college to accommodate adequately, for the first time, the ten faculty and 700 students who by that year made up the Fine Arts Department. William and Mary could at last offer the fine arts curriculum that Thomas Jefferson had envisioned in 1779, and which Leslie Cheek had done much to help realize.

Cheek's growing repute also put him in demand for other design assignments. In 1938 he was appointed to Virginia's Art Commission, which passed judgment on state-funded art and architectural projects. He also headed up Virginia's team of four designers who created the "Virginia Room" for the 1939 New York World's Fair. His collaborators were fellow William and Mary faculty members Edwin Rust, Leonard Haber and Arthur Ross, a lighting specialist.

Their concept was a serene sitting room where weary fair-goers could rest amid soothing colors. The room's centerpiece was a bubbling fountain, topped by Rust's contemporary sculpture symbolizing Virginia's rivers. Bookcases were filled with albums of Virginia photographs, all carefully labeled, and refreshments were served in an atmosphere of relaxed hospitality.

But by 1939 an era was coming to a close, both for Williamsburg and the nation. The wonderful four years of "Brigadoon," as Jim Cogar called Williamsburg, were ending for Leslie Cheek and his staff at the college. No more argumentative fine arts lunches, no more all-night scene-building to meet a play's opening night. When the dance floors and lanterns which Leslie Cheek had designed were installed in their usual places in the Sunken Garden in June 1939, Leslie himself had gone. He was on his way to a new and larger world.

President Bryan summed up the magical effect of Cheek's four short years:

The peculiar value of Mr. Cheek's work at the College of William and Mary has been in his perception of the irreplaceable importance of art in college life today. Not art only as a field for amateurs, but art as a field for intelligent and trained appreciation; art as a medium of self-expression and, above all, in the long years of leisure that lie ahead, art as a source of fuller culture, and as a stimulus to continuous growth . . .

A deepening of life and a widening of horizons must be aims of growth. Those purposes Mr. Cheek appreciated, and under his leadership notable progress has been made towards their attainment . . .   □

The Baltimore Museum of Art was designed by John Russell Pope. Located near Johns Hopkins University, the municipal art gallery opened in 1914. Cheek was named director in 1939, a post he held for nearly three years.

CHAPTER V

The Baltimore Years

Leslie and Mary Tyler were married in Richmond on June 3, 1939. Here the newlyweds emerge from Mabel Cheek's 1936 Lincoln town car at the reception held at Westbourne, the Freeman family's home.

Leslie Cheek married Mary Tyler Freeman on June 3, 1939, on a sultry Saturday afternoon. Even in Richmond, a church-centered city of big family weddings, it was a splendid affair. Bishop James Edward Freeman of the Episcopal Diocese of Washington, D.C., conducted the service in St. Stephen's Church. In the wedding party were Mary Tyler's sister Anne as well as Leslie's sister Huldah, and his friends Jim Cogar and Ed Frost. Heading a contingent of Cheeks and Tennessee friends was Mabel Cheek, who came by train, since her Lincoln town car was to be used in the wedding. After a reception in the Freemans' garden at Westbourne, their house in the Westhampton suburbs, the couple spent a quiet week at Cheekwood before beginning their six-week honeymoon in California and Hawaii.

The first weeks after their arrival in Baltimore, the couple devoted themselves to moving into the Warrington, a staid and capacious apartment building full of wealthy widows, located within easy walking distance of the Baltimore Museum.

Mary Tyler, with the help of servants Helen and Dunlop Jones, brought along from Williamsburg, supervised the moving of furniture and the uncrating of wedding gifts. "The moving job was enormous," she recalled years later. Leslie had redesigned their 12th floor apartment in the then-popular Art Deco style, and its fresh and original appearance attracted immediate attention. An *Interiors Magazine* article praised Cheek's design for its careful blending of comfort and elegance in a contemporary motif.

During the first several weeks, Leslie was confronted with two challenges: acquainting himself with the museum, its staff and its holdings; and preparing the galleries for *Art of the Medici*, the museum's previously-planned exhibit, which was the first in Cheek's directorship.

Housed in a handsome building designed by John Russell Pope on the edge of the Johns

At The Warrington in Baltimore the Cheeks rented a twelfth-floor apartment, overlooking the city.

ABOVE: Mary Tyler enjoyed caring for plants, so Leslie added this "garden" to the living room at the Warrington. **RIGHT:** Cheek designed this large dining table which featured removable panels at its center. The flowers are lit from below, and by a row of ceiling fixtures. Leonard Haber created the wall paintings. The study at the Baltimore apartment had a Cheek-designed desk. The Art-Deco inspired piece is still in use today in the library at the Cheeks' Richmond home.

Hopkins University campus, the Baltimore Museum owned too few valuable art works to attract many visitors. It was typical of the smaller fine arts museums of its time—a stolid institution which depended largely on its permanent collection to attract visitors. The new director recognized solutions at once. First, "The Baltimore Museum had to develop a role for itself," he concluded. "I began to hold loan exhibitions with elaborate explanations, often organized around a central theme . . ." Through use of frequently changing displays, Cheek aimed to increase both the museum's offerings and the public interest.

Cheek's second move was to seize the opportunity presented by the growth of leisure time—a relatively new phenomenon in a nation so ardently dedicated to the work ethic. There could be no denying that changes in life- and work-styles formalized by the New Deal's 40-hour work week left Americans with time on their hands, and Cheek wanted them to fill their spare time at the art museum.

But how to get them in?

Cheek decided art had to be made fun. "Too many people leave art museums slightly discouraged, though they probably never will admit it," he told the *Baltimore Sun* on Septem-

More Fun Per Masterpiece . . .

Richard Q. Yardley, the *Baltimore Sun* cartoonist, humorously heralded a new age at the city's art museum under its new director. This drawing appeared in the newspaper shortly before Leslie assumed his post. (Courtesy: *Baltimore Sun*)

ber 4, 1939. "A museum just seems to give a person who isn't acquainted with art an inferiority complex."

Twenty-five years later, when he was director of the Virginia Museum of Fine Arts in Richmond, Cheek reminisced about his early ideas concerning the arts: "During my second year at Harvard I transferred from engineering to fine arts, and I took all the wonderful courses they offered. The art museum is a wonderful institution. But I kept asking myself, 'If it is all so wonderful, then why don't more people enjoy it and understand it? If art is so ennobling and so uplifting, how can more people get to understand it?'"

Believing that most museums were "pretty stuffy places," Cheek hit upon the idea of making a visit to the museum an entertaining experience by applying the techniques of theatre design he had acquired at Yale to exhibition installation. "There's more to running a museum than hanging some pictures and waiting for people to come see them," he told a newspaperman shortly after becoming director. "It's a good idea to use all the new inventions at our command to interest the people of the city in exhibits."

Along with a commitment to theatricality, Leslie Cheek had a more serious intention: to make art a part of life, not just a diversion. Museum president Henry Treide, in announcing Cheek's appointment, best summed up this objective: "Mr. Cheek's main theory—that art should be an integral part of every person's life and not just a subject taught critically in schools and thereafter never thought of or practiced—closely parallels the new [museum] policy to bring art into the life of every citizen of Baltimore. Mr. Cheek [at William and Mary] drew [students] into activity which led to close association with all art forms, starting with the premise that most students in colleges today learn how to make a living but not how to live, that most leisure time is wasted by the average person, and that the fine arts should remedy both of these situations if presented properly . . ."

To Cheek, vivid imagery and dramatic

setting achieved by theatre designers through the manipulation of lighting, texture, color, music and even smell, could be applied with equal success to art exhibitions to engage the curious. Information about what was being looked at would be conveyed on wall panels. The idea was for the museum-goer to walk through the pages of a book, with the eye delighted and the mind engaged.

Art of the Medici gave Cheek the first opportunity to weave his magic, and he wanted this exhibit to exemplify the changes he intended to introduce. The museum's staff worked over-time to transform the building into a Renaissance *palazzo*. Its central court, heretofore empty and forbidding, was gaily festooned with garlands of fruit, and on its walls were hung Renaissance masterpieces borrowed from the Metropolitan, Fogg and Cleveland museums, as well as from a host of private collections.

Intermixed with the paintings were examples of 16th century decorative arts and sculpture, plus tapestries and suits of armor. The careful placement of spotlights lit the objects with wondrous effect. To bring the era of the Medici to life, Cheek arranged for an evening of dance and song, with the performers arrayed in 16th century finery. One almost expected Lorenzo the Magnificent himself to emerge from the museum's shadows. And everywhere were to be found large partitions covered with text—explaining the era, the Medici family and the artists.

Art of the Medici proved a triumphant success. The gala evening opening attracted a record crowd of 1,800 people, resplendent in their best evening attire. Wrote the *Sun,* the exhibit is "entirely different from anything yet shown in Baltimore or in Washington. It is a progressive and provocative example of modern museum presentation."

The new director's first season elicited further innovations. For *Modern Painting Isms and How they Grew,* Cheek disguised a museum guard to look like his 19th century counterpart at the Louvre in Paris. This character, complete with false whiskers and frock coat,

BELOW: Scheduled before his appointment as director, *Art of the Medici* was Cheek's first Baltimore exhibition. The museum's central hall was turned into an Italian renaissance court, decorated with garlands of fruit and filled with art objects from the period. **RIGHT:** Information panels, here a map of 16th century Florence, were among Cheek's innovations at Baltimore. He wanted gallery visitors to feel that they were walking through a book describing the history of Renaissance Italy.

ABOVE: A Baltimore Museum guard, disguised as his 19th century counterpart at Paris' Louvre. He patrolled a replica of a *salon* as part of *Modern Painting Isms and How They Grew.* Putting guards in costume was one of Cheek's favorite devices. It was his way of saying art should be fun. RIGHT: The French *salon* recreated for *Modern Painting Isms,* which was held in 1940.

was to patrol a replica of a Louvre gallery which featured the works of academic painters, and was encouraged to pinch lady visitors. It was Cheek's off-beat way of recreating another time and place. He even provided a small *salon* and book collection at the end of the exhibition of over 170 Cubist, Primitivist, Surrealist and Post-Impressionist paintings, where visitors could argue—albeit quietly— about which "Ism" was superior.

The notion of involving the public with the art on the walls was carried yet another step with *Art Begins at Home,* an exhibition devoted to the good design of affordable household objects. With the aid of John Koenig, a brilliant designer from Yale who had joined the museum in January, 1940, Cheek provided a maze at the show's entrance. Upon entering the exhibition, visitors were confronted by cubicles each with two everyday objects, say two clocks or two radios, and were to select which of the pair they thought was the better designed. Above each object was an arrow which the visitor was to follow after making his or her choice. If the "wrong" or poorly-designed object was selected, the museum-goer ended up in a *cul de sac,* which featured an explanation of why the item failed to embody sound principals of design. Some people found the maze so bewildering that they got lost in it and had to be guided out. Yet no matter how strange Baltimoreans found Cheek's installation, *Art Begins at Home* left a lasting impression.

The Cheek formula reached its apogee with *Romanticism in America,* the subject of which was the state of American taste in the United States from 1812 to 1865. *Romanticism,* which closed out Cheek's first season in June of 1940, brought to life the era of the Gothic Revival, of Stephen Foster and of crinoline and lace, through a masterful blending of art, theatre and music. The galleries were a virtual textbook through which visitors wandered, tracing the origins of the Romantic movement, and its unforgettable influence on painting, literature, architecture and fashion.

Cheek's staff located the long-lost script

The maze (below) at the entrance to *Art Begins at Home.* Patrons can be seen selecting the better designed example from displays of household objects (above).

In the summer of 1940 Mrs. John D. Rockefeller, Jr., asked Leslie to help create an anti-totalitarian, pro-democratic display for the Museum of Modern Art entitled *For Us the Living*. The proposed exhibition was intended to warn Americans about the dangers of isolationism. In the end, a lack of funds for the ambitious plan prevented its execution. (Courtesy: Rockefeller Center Management Corporation, New York)

Cheek's most ambitious exhibition at Baltimore was *Romanticism in America*, mounted there in 1940. Included were displays of 19th century painting, sculpture and fashion. A costume ball was held at which guests wore romantic period dress. The museum also staged *The Six Degrees of Crime*, first performed just prior to the Civil War. By integrating the static and the performing arts, Cheek brought the past to life. One newspaper called the exhibition "unfailingly entertaining and distinctly amusing."

of *The Six Degrees of Crime*, a sentimental morality play first performed in Boston in 1837, which was dusted off and presented anew in the museum's tiny basement auditorium. The once-quiet museum took on the appearance of Margaret Mitchell's "Tara," when it became the site for "Godey's Ball and Entertainment." Guests donned 19th century costumes, some of them family heirlooms, and danced waltzes, polkas and gavottes while musicians from the Peabody Conservatory played from a gay bandstand late into the evening.

Romanticism was such a hit that its run was extended beyond its scheduled July closing through the end of August. Wrote a *Sun* reviewer: "It is beyond all doubt the outstanding display of the season . . . I cannot offhand think of any Baltimore exhibit of the past which has been more thoughtfully organized and more brilliantly set out for public view." The reviewer felt the "museum has carried out an ambitious and difficult task in a manner that is astonishingly successful . . . [It] has made a first rate addition to our sense of the past and to our respect for its potency in our own environment." Indeed, in an informal poll conducted by the museum, Baltimoreans overwhelmingly selected *Medici* and *Romanticism* as the most outstanding shows of 1939-40.

Flush with success after his first season, Leslie joined Mary Tyler, now expecting their first child, for a July vacation in Vermont. However, the tranquility was to prove short-lived when Cheek received a telephone call from Abby Aldrich Rockefeller, whom he had known in Williamsburg. She told him that the trustees of the Museum of Modern Art in New York, which she had helped create, wanted him to design a special exhibit to be housed at MOMA—possibly in an addition. She described in broad terms what was wanted: a dramatic display intended to warn the complacent American public of the late-1930s about the dangers posed to democracy by the totalitarian regimes of Germany and Italy. Intrigued, Cheek immediately agreed to undertake this project for which his talents

Cheek's 1940 sketch for the "Avenue of Fascism," for the Museum of Modern Art exhibit. Nazi-saluting robots lined the walls while martial music blared in the unrealized plan.

seemed so ideally suited. Abby's son, Nelson, later governor of New York and vice-president of the United States, arranged for the Baltimore Museum to grant its director leave to work in New York on the MOMA exhibition.

Leslie then cut short his vacation, and moved to Manhattan's Dorset Hotel. In due course he was joined by urbanist Lewis Mumford, architect Edward Durell Stone, MOMA's director Alfred Barr, and his assistant John Abbott. This team worked diligently to create a scenario entitled *For Us the Living*. Inspired by some of the technical feats achieved at the New York World's Fair (still open in the summer of 1940), the group proposed exposing the exhibition's visitors to a series of sound and light experiences which would forcefully make the case for preserving democratic principals—i.e. "the American way"—against the threats of barbarism and enslavement presented by Hitler and Mussolini.

Leslie and Mary Tyler with Dr. and Mrs. Douglas Southall Freeman attend a formal dinner at Cheekwood, 1940. This photo was taken in the living room of the mansion.

Proud parents show their first-born, Leslie Cheek III, in the nursery at the Baltimore apartment.

The Cone Apartment Model Room at the Baltimore Museum of Art reproduces Etta Cone's Eutaw Place quarters which were jammed with Matisses and Picassos. (The Baltimore Museum of Art: This room was created through the generosity of Cone family members. Given in memory of Laura & Julius Cone by their children.)

However, their elaborate plan would have been so expensive to implement, that its cost simply staggered potential backers. Support for *For Us the Living* evaporated. Mumford was furious, believing the team had been caught up in MOMA's serpentine inside politics. He felt the team had been "ditched, deliberately sidetracked." Sharing his colleague's feelings, but not stating them openly, Cheek returned to Baltimore mystified and disappointed.

Back at the Baltimore Museum, the director was concerned with more than assembling a succession of temporary shows, dazzling though they might be. He also had to think about the museum's permanent holdings. Recognizing the need for a stronger collection, Cheek set to work to cultivate potential local donors of art works. One was the celebrated collector Etta Cone, who had amassed one of the world's largest private collections of Matisses and Picassos. Her two Marlborough apartments on Baltimore's Eutaw Place were jammed with art. Even the kitchen and bathroom were hung with modern masters! Yet Cheek was not a lonely suitor, for one day while on a visit to "Miss Etta," Cheek ran into MOMA's Alfred Barr who was equally determined to have the Cone collection part of *his* museum. Eventually, Etta Cone left it to the Baltimore Museum, and though this gift came several years after Leslie Cheek had resigned the directorship to enter the Army, one cannot doubt her action was the result of his skillful persuasion.

In October of 1940, the museum opened a beautifully-lit, oak-paneled Jacobean room with ancient fireplace and authentic 17th century objects. The room, donated by Miss Saidi May, had originally been part of a manor house in Shrewsbury, England.

The museum also had a small basement auditorium, and a nascent theatre program, directed by the hard-working Kay Rockefeller

(no kin to the benefactors of Colonial Williamsburg). Cheek was determined to make the theatre a more important part of his overall plan for the museum, and in 1940 he succeeded in obtaining $200,000 from the Rockefellers' General Education Board in New York to permit at least one theatre event each season related to a museum exhibition. Cheek named Katherine Rivett to head this project, asking her to enlist the volunteer services of local actors, dancers, designers, musicians and technicians to assist the museum's small staff.

In these austere years, the museum budget remained slim, but volunteers from Johns Hopkins, the Peabody Conservatory, the Junior League and other organizations played a crucial role. The museum theatre's first production was Eugene O'Neill's *The Long Voyage Home*. Another more controversial play was *One Third of a Nation*, which documented the impact of the Depression on the American people. Observing the effect of the theatre in drawing viewers to the gallery, Cheek became convinced that any well-equipped art museum needed a stage—and the most technically up-to-date, at that. This insight was to play a part in his Richmond career years later.

Other Baltimore additions reflected Cheek's endless imagination and inventiveness. To stimulate the interest of children, he designed and installed in the museum's grim basement, a replica of an ancient Egyptian tomb, complete with mummy and sarcophogus. To encourage visitation, Cheek oversaw the installation of a Members' Room, where patrons could enjoy afternoon tea. The young director also initiated regular film, music and lecture series.

A stream of Cheek's loan exhibitions continued to move in and out of the museum's galleries. The sheer variety of topics had Baltimoreans scratching their heads in disbelief. Museum visitors found out that art did not consist just of paintings and sculpture, but also industrial design, furniture design, movie-making, even city planning and weaponry of a world then at war.

A firm believer in making art museums a showplace for both the static and performing arts, Cheek initiated theatre productions in the small basement auditorium at the Baltimore Museum. The political overtones of *One Third of a Nation* (above) made it one of the more controversial presentations staged at the museum.

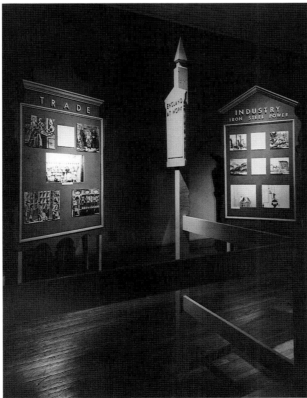

Information panels such as these for *Georgian England* were a feature at Cheek's exhibitions. They helped explain to museum-goers the era and historical conditions which produced the art they had come to see. Note also the use of dramatic lighting to illuminate these panels. At Baltimore, and later at the Virginia Museum, Cheek put to use his extensive training in theatre and lighting design.

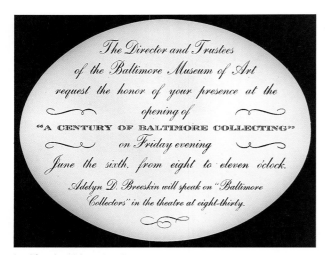

As Cheek said at the time, "This display is a tribute to a fine past, and . . . an inspiration toward an even finer future." This 19th century-styled invitation was mailed to each member of the Baltimore Museum.

THE ★ BALTIMORE ★ MUSEUM ★ OF ★ ART
presents

DESIGN DECADE

in
RADIO ★ FILM ★ THEATRE ★ DANCE

The invitation to the Baltimore Museum exhibition, *Design Decade*. This show offered an examination of contemporary industrial design, as well as performing arts including dance, film, theatre and radio.

The City was another attempt by Cheek to integrate the arts—in this case city planning—with life. The exhibition featured the model of a futuristic city from the General Motors Pavilion at the 1939 World's Fair.

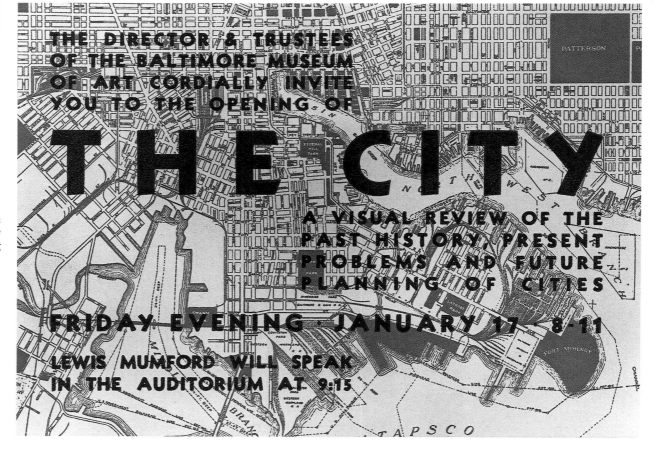

86

The New York World's Fair (1939-40) with its modern architectural impact was clearly reflected in *The City*. It opened at the museum in January 1941, and was held in conjunction with public discussion of a newly introduced plan for the future course of Baltimore's growth. The exhibition included the model of "The City of the Future" which had so amazed World's Fair visitors at General Motors' "Futurama," with its prognostications—accurate as it turned out—of multilane freeways and towering glass skyscrapers. Cheek arranged for his friend Lewis Mumford, the famed chronicler of the development of urban America, to deliver a lecture on the city in American culture.

Cranbrook's Carl Milles was the subject of another exhibition. Finished plaster casts of the sculptor's works were assembled in the museum's spacious columned central court and were illumined with warm spotlights before blue green gauze hung in folds from the ceiling to imitate water. The *Baltimore Sun* called it the "most comprehensive and authoritative of all exhibits of . . . Milles . . . The city has had a leading part in assembling and the first chance to see this display of an artist . . . ranked with the greatest sculptors of modern times."

Indeed, the exhibition was the largest to feature Milles' work ever held and the most significant since Milles emigrated to the United States from Sweden in 1931. Milles himself told museum members that he had never before seen such an effective display of his works. Following his speech, the museum presented a ballet, *The Marriage of Rivers*, which interpreted Milles' recently-completed fountain in St. Louis depicting the joining of the Missouri and Mississippi rivers.

From the beginning, Leslie Cheek's career in Baltimore had been clouded by the prospect of war. Indeed, at the same moment Cheek was to assume the directorship, Germany's *blitzkreig* had flattened Poland. The summer of 1940 had brought a series of daring German U-boat attacks against British and American shipping off the Atlantic coast—one

This display showed Baltimoreans that art included more than painting and sculpture, and also embraced industrial design—the creation of useful and beautiful objects for day-to-day use in the modern world. *Design Decade* was one of many traveling shows organized by New York's Museum of Modern Art which visited Baltimore.

of them within sight of bathers at Virginia Beach—and seemed to portend to Cheek the possibility of U-boat shellings of Baltimore and other port cities. Soon, the couple found themselves participating in air raid drills, and curtained their windows during so-called blackouts. "Art seems a trivial thing to talk about when one thinks of what is happening abroad," Leslie told a *Sun* reporter.

Appropriately, in October 1940 the museum mounted *Again: Arms and Armor*, illustrating the development of military weapons and their effects on history, science and art.

Not surprisingly, the pervasive war fever made it a highly popular show; however, Cheek was quick to deny any propagandistic intent. "In presenting this exhibition, the museum is aligning itself with neither isolationists, nor pro-war factions," he said. To display the panoply of weapons, borrowed mostly from New York's Metropolitan Museum, the galleries were blacked out, and crossbows, lances, guns and airplane models were bathed in eerie spotlights.

Following the attack on Pearl Harbor on December 7, 1941, Leslie was determined to

LEFT: The work of Carl Milles, one of Cheek's favorite sculptors, was the subject of another exhibition held at the Baltimore Museum. These plaster casts were illuminated with pink spotlights in the dimly lit gallery. To imitate falling water, blue-green gauze was hung in the background. **BELOW:** Included in the 1940 Milles exhibition was a performance of *The Marriage of the Rivers*, a ballet based on the Swedish artist's well-known sculpture of the same title located in St. Louis, Missouri.

Cheek at work. Some of his most satisfying moments were spent at this drawing board where he created many designs for museum exhibitions as well as sketches for Faraway Farm, and later Skylark Farm, the Cheek family's two rural retreats.

enter military service without delay. As the Navy had no immediate need for his services, he offered his talents to the Army. John Stewart Bryan urged the Special Service Command in Washington to use his abilities. Doctor Freeman advised his son-in-law to follow the example of General Lee and sign up with the Corps of Engineers. Finally, in May of 1942, after what seemed an eternity of evasions and delays, Cheek was commissioned a captain in the Army Engineers and ordered to report to Fort Belvoir, Virginia.

Cheek immediately tendered his resignation after two years as director of a museum he had done so much to enliven. Museum attendance had jumped nearly 200,000 over the preceding period. The city greatly upped its museum support. Some art objects plus an unusual period interior and a Members' Room had been added. More importantly, the

young director had raised the public's perception of what had once been a rather quiet art museum.

In its February 1940 issue, *Forum and Century Magazine* ran a highly critical article on "Elegant Indigence in Baltimore." Writing in the murderous vein of Baltimore's own H. L. Mencken, the author, Audrey Granneberg, observed that "Except perhaps for Boston, [Baltimore] is perhaps the smuggest city in America." But in this culturally inert environment, she declared, "The Municipal Art Museum is a rare exception to the general stagnation" of their city. "Baltimoreans enjoy their museum and are rightly proud of it," she concluded.

In a farewell editorial on May 12, 1942, as Cheek entered military service, the admiring *Sun* declared, "He has injected tremendous vitality into the Art Museum . . . Therefore, one can only lament his departure." The paper continued:

> Mr. Cheek's innovations at the museum have not been approved universally; some of them, indeed, have been denounced with ferocity. But the very fact that he could stir up a fight is conclusive proof that he engaged the interest of the public; whatever else the museum may have been under his administration, it was not a mausoleum of dead art. On the contrary, it was one of the liveliest institutions in Baltimore. Whether you liked it or disliked it, you always kept your eye on it, for something was always happening there.

It was significant that Leslie did not ask the museum for a leave, but resigned outright. He felt he had done what he could for the institution. He was not sure what he faced at war's end, but this gifted and self-assured son of Mabel Cheek was confident that the good fortune that had led him to Williamsburg and then to Baltimore would continue to look out for him. The future was something he could not be troubled over, for, at the moment, his chief concern was to help win the war that threatened both America and the freedoms under which the arts could flourish. □

Faraway Farm, Lake Lure, North Carolina. On the eve of World War II, Cheek conceived this house as a haven for his family. The residence (left), suggested by designs of Frank Lloyd Wright, overlooks the rapids of Buffalo Creek. Behind the house (right) were guest quarters and a garage. (Painting by William Bailey, Lynchburg, Virginia)

CHAPTER VI

The War and New York

When Leslie Cheek resigned from the Baltimore Museum in May of 1942, Germany was ravaging Europe and the Japanese seemed to be in command in the Pacific. Like most men his age—33—he desperately wanted to take up the fight. Even so, he worried that his art background had ill-prepared him for any useful role. "My training seems apparently useless to the country," he wrote a Nashville friend after the Navy had rejected him, "and I worry a good deal about my inadequacy."

However, his worries proved unfounded when the Army Corps of Engineers assigned him to Fort Belvoir, close to Virginia's historic Mount Vernon. A month after being inducted he wrote his wife, "My going into the Army, of course, is a great change for me. The full course of my career has been stopped, and the future is completely unknown. But these are the times in which we live—and we must live honorably and bravely. I am only lucky to get into work somewhat fitting my training." Like thousands of other young men who suddenly found themselves crowded into military camps, he found Army procedures disorganized and impersonal. "[O]ne feels completely lost in the cogs of a great machine, with an unknown 'they' deciding your particular and unimportant fate."

At first Captain Cheek lived in barracks at Fort Belvoir, but later moved to an English basement apartment in Washington when he was assigned to the Office of the Chief of Engineers. Here he was the assistant to a pompous colonel who spent most of his time flying from one Engineer's base to another—to collect extra flight pay from the Army, Cheek suspected. The post involved a monotonous routine of shuffling paperwork on top of more paperwork, and witnessing endless maneuverings associated with office politics. He became convinced his work had nothing to do with winning the war, and he hoped for a transfer.

While her husband endured office boredom, Mary Tyler, now expecting their second child, divided her time between visits to her parents' Richmond home and moving into the recently completed Faraway Farm, near Asheville, North Carolina.

Faraway Farm grew out of Leslie's fears for his family's safety. The threat of German bombardment of American cities seemed very real at the time. The vulnerability of Baltimore, so near the Atlantic coast, was underscored by the city's repeated air raid drills. Convinced of the need for a haven for his wife and infant son, Leslie III, born in December of 1940, Leslie began the search for an isolated spot on which to build a farm which no enemy would threaten.

As a boy he had vacationed with his family at Grove Park Inn near Asheville, and the locale seemed to offer what Cheek was looking for: a remote area in a beautiful setting. In the summer of 1940, he persuaded his friend Stewart Bryan, son of the William and Mary

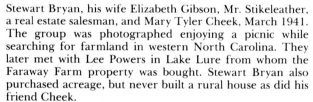

Stewart Bryan, his wife Elizabeth Gibson, Mr. Stikeleather, a real estate salesman, and Mary Tyler Cheek, March 1941. The group was photographed enjoying a picnic while searching for farmland in western North Carolina. They later met with Lee Powers in Lake Lure from whom the Faraway Farm property was bought. Stewart Bryan also purchased acreage, but never built a rural house as did his friend Cheek.

ABOVE RIGHT: The living-dining room at Faraway Farm. This room reflects Cheek's high regard for contemporary furnishings. Large windows provided natural lighting and sweeping views of the rugged countryside which surrounded the farmhouse. **RIGHT:** Sofas converted into beds in the guest room at Faraway. The fireplace was the only source of heat in this room located in a dependency behind the main house. (Reprinted by permission of *House Beautiful,* copyright © June 1951. The Hearst Corp. All Rights Reserved. Rodney McCay Morgan, photographer.)

94

president, to go with him to Lake Lure, 25 miles southeast of Asheville. They met with Lee Powers, a real estate salesman and contractor who showed them properties available for sale.

The two men were so impressed with the area's tranquil isolation that they returned with their wives, whose similar enthusiasm led Cheek and Bryan to form the Chebry Corporation, and to purchase about 3,000 acres of land, then relatively inexpensive.

Leslie selected the site for his Faraway Farm residence about a mile and a half from the shore of Lake Lure, on a bluff overlooking the rushing waters of Buffalo Creek. Baltimore architect Henry Scarff was engaged to prepare working drawings based on Cheek's own tracings. The handsome farmhouse was built of wood, stained a pleasant gray to imitate the weathered coloration of local farm buildings, complemented by fieldstone masonry in steps, chimneys and terraces. The building had a modern simplicity about it, plus style and comfort, and was nestled among bounteous natural growths of mountain laurel, rhododendron and dogwood.

In later years, Leslie referred to it as "my Frank Lloyd Wright house." With the help of Lee Powers, who was to become an indispensable adviser and trusted friend, Cheek installed a gravity-powered water system connecting the house and outbuildings to a nearby spring, improved the virtually nonexistent road to the house, and brought in electric power and, eventually, a telephone.

Faraway Farm was one of the creative delights of Cheek's early manhood. It gave him his first opportunity to design a house of his own, including its interiors and furnishings, as well as its gardens. He wanted it to be a sort of Shangri-La for him, his wife and growing family. It had five bedrooms and four baths, a large living-dining room, plus a study, kitchen, pantry and servant quarters. Eventually it also had a guest house, auto and machinery shelters, and a barn with a cow. A boathouse was built at the Lake, and a pony was bought for the children.

Mary Tyler and her daughter Elizabeth watch the *Sadie Belle* approach the family boathouse on Lake Lure. (Reprinted by permission of *House Beautiful*, copyright © June 1951. The Hearst Corp. All Rights Reserved. Rodney McCay Morgan, photographer.)

Leslie, an officer in the Corps of Engineers, and his mother, photographed during one of his rare wartime visits to Faraway Farm. Cheek's Army duties in Washington prevented his making frequent trips to North Carolina.

Mabel Cheek provided these boxwood which line the garden entrance walk to the farmhouse. In the distance is the barn. During the war, Mary Tyler ran a profitable egg-producing business with the help of Lee Powers.

They also planned for it to be a partly self-sustaining farm with cattle and chickens, fruit trees and vegetable garden. In fact, Mary Tyler made the egg operation a profit-making enterprise during the war. She was assisted by Lee Powers, a full-time caretaker, as well as a steady stream of "Army wives" who would join her for visits which would last weeks at a time. Mary Tyler stayed only during the summer months at the farm, spending the rest of the year either with her parents or at a house which she and her husband rented in Washington.

Thus Faraway Farm provided the harbor of safety that Leslie envisioned. As he wrote Mary Tyler in June of 1942, "The Army sends you wherever and whenever it chooses. I am more thankful everyday for our 'base' at Faraway. With so much uncertainty, this *surety* is deeply satisfying."

Captain Cheek's prayers for a transfer out of the Chief of Engineers Office were answered in late 1942 when he was told to report back to Fort Belvoir to head the Camouflage Training Section of the Army Engineers School. He was soon promoted to Major. "The Camouflage course is badly organized, but interesting," he wrote Mary Tyler. "It *could* be *so much* better, though. The Army's standard of teaching is naive, slow and awkward."

His restless, critical mind went immediately to work to revamp the Army's obviously old-fashioned camouflage teaching methods, which had changed little since World War I. Calling on his arts training, Cheek developed new visual training aids to teach soldiers how to disguise themselves and their equipment from enemy detection.

The first order of business was to completely revise the Army's single vintage camouflage training manual. "With luck I was able to persuade the Engineers' authorities to issue a series of fresh new manuals with well-conceived layouts," he recalled years later. "I had great help from Major Jo Meilziner and Lieutenant Joseph Krush," the former having been a leading New York stage designer in the

pre-war years. Realistic color illustrations replaced black and white diagrams. Among Belvoir's soldiers he found skilled writers to prepare the manuals' texts.

With the aid of Lieutenant David Yerkes, a Yale architecture graduate, Major Cheek transformed the base's old and obsolete riding hall into a camouflage training center.

Cheek was not above employing novel techniques to liven up the training sessions. Yerkes remembered that "Leslie prepared a series of slides for use in lectures. In order to keep the audience awake, he arranged to include slides of a voluptuous model named Chili Williams. These were worked in with the others at odd intervals in hopes that no one would doze off for fear of missing something. I believe it was Leslie's hope that Chili could be shown nude, but this was too racey for the Corps of Engineers." The slide series was appropriately called "Conceal or Reveal."

Indeed, Chili was such a popular addition to the training program that Major Cheek passed out packets of glossy photos of the vivacious model, along with forbidden cigars, to soldiers who had attained high marks in his courses. The post commandant was nonplussed at the sight of troops unceremoniously puffing away on their newly-acquired stogies.

After the birth of Douglas Freeman Cheek in January of 1943, Mary Tyler joined her husband, who was now clearly relishing his role as an instructor, at a house they rented on 34th Place, near the National Cathedral. A year later, they found a larger house on Leroy Place, between Connecticut Avenue and California Street, and remained there until the war's end.

The Cheeks found their life in Washington growing livelier as they rediscovered old friends now engaged in civilian and military jobs. Yale and Harvard friends—such as Leonard Haber and David Yerkes—made living in the war-time capital convivial. Once at a party Cheek and Yerkes noticed that most of the other, more experienced officers present had many ribbons on their uniforms, whereas

As head of the Camouflage Section of the Engineer School at Fort Belvoir from 1942-44, Major Cheek devised fresh and often unorthodox training techniques for officers and enlisted men.

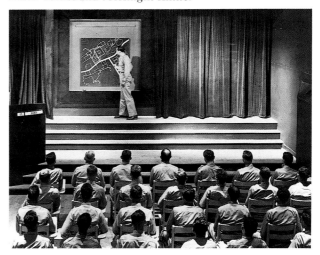

Lt. Leonard Haber lectures on camouflage in what was once an Army cavalry unit's riding hall at Ft. Belvoir, ca. 1943. Other Yale graduates on Cheek's military staff included David Yerkes and McKnight Kinne.

IN CAMOUFLAGE

Shadows

REVEAL OR CONCEAL

Since soldiers in his classes often went to sleep during lectures, Cheek inserted racey slides of models to illustrate camouflage lessons, such as this view of the then-popular pin-up Chili Williams. (Ewing Krainin, *Life Magazine,* © 1944 Time Inc.)

Cheek persuaded the Corps of Engineers to use full-color illustrations in World War II camouflage training booklets issued by the Army.

98

CAMOUFLAGE OF MACHINE GUNS

FIGURE 53.—*Close-up of hasty emplacement for heavy MG.*

A machine gun in the front line is under enemy observation on the ground and from the air. The position may be hasty, using natural materials only to gain concealment; it may be dug-in, with a flat-top; or it may be a relatively permanent position, dug-in more carefully, also with a flat-top.

In certain situations, protection from enemy ground observation is the most important requirement. As the position is improved, camouflage measures are taken to afford protection from aerial observation as well. To check concealment from the ground, squad leaders should examine all machine-gun positions from the direction of the enemy to check on individual camouflage, as suggested in FM 7-10. In the case of dug-in and relatively permanent positions, the concealment must deceive enemy observation both on the ground and in the air.

When used on antiaircraft mounts, machine guns may be in hastily prepared positions on the surface of the ground; or in more deliberate dug-in positions with flat-tops. When they form a part of light or heavy antiaircraft positions near the front lines, they are subject to enemy observation by reconnaissance and tank patrols. When they are a part of bivouacs or other rear-area installations, protection only from enemy aerial observers may be necessary.

Though front-line concealment of machine guns and their crews varies with the type of position and weapon, the following discussion with illustrations may suggest solutions typical of front-line problems.

In certain situations, hasty machine-gun nests must be protected from enemy ground observation from the front and from both flanks (fig. 53). Choice of site depends on the mission. Note that this nest blends with the natural foliage background. Shadows of adjacent bushes add to concealment. Spoil from a hasty emplacement of this type must be covered with sod saved from the emplacement top, supplemented by natural materials (fig. 54). Ammunition and empty cartridge cases are hidden behind and beneath natural materials to prevent reflections attracting enemy eyes.

The crew must avoid silhouette against the skyline. The only movement permitted is movement essential to performing the mission. Soldiers' faces should be toned down to prevent shine. Natural materials on helmets would also help to blend soldiers with background.

The layout shown in figure 55 provides access, behind cover and well concealed, for the ammunition carriers.

In the circle in figure 56 the same nest is shown, as viewed by the enemy. Note that concealment depends on blending with background, spoil hidden or concealed with natural materials, use of shadows, and prevention of shine or reflections.

In the diagonal view from the front of a hasty emplacement for a light machine gun, a flat-top is illustrated (fig. 57). Natural materials have been removed from the front of the position and used to garnish the net. Machine-gun crews should clear away enough natural materials to obtain a clear field of fire, leaving a thin natural screen to help conceal the characteristic black line at the

32

33

they had none. Thinking quickly, Cheek found two brightly colored pot holders which the two ostentatiously pinned to their chests.

"We were fortunate to have help throughout the war," Mary Tyler says now. "We had a cook, Hester; a maid, Fay; and an English nurse during the first year. In the second year we had to let the British nanny go because she was too mean. We had many wonderful friends. In fact, I often felt guilty that we were having such a fascinating time when so many people we knew were in danger and separated from those dearest to them . . . Altogether, I worked as a nurse's aide and divided my time between my friends and children."

After two years at Belvoir, Cheek was ordered to the Office of Strategic Services in Washington, at the direction of General William "Wild Bill" Donovan, the former Wall Street lawyer who headed America's espionage activities. One of Donovan's assistants was sent to Fort Belvoir to obtain the transfer of a group of Engineers officers trained in strategic camouflage. This group, with Leslie as its head, was slated to be attached to the staff of Admiral Lord Louis Mountbatten, who commanded the Allies' South East Asia Command. The American engineers were to report to Ceylon to train Mountbatten's contingent of native troops in concealment as part of an operational camouflage mission against Japanese occupation forces concentrated at Singapore and Rangoon. As it turned out, the British cancelled American participation in the Far Eastern offensive. Major Cheek remained in the OSS, however he never went overseas.

He underwent vigorous field training at a rural camp near Leesburg, Virginia, under a British major named Fairbairn. Included were courses in spy techniques. One of them required Cheek to react instantly with his .45 calibre pistol whenever a mechanical target popped up, simulating the enemy. In another course he was required to reconnoitre an enemy town (actually Leesburg) and then draw from memory detailed charts of its streets and landmarks, showing its best targets and providing the silhouettes and estimated heights of its buildings.

But Cheek proved not to be spy material, so after his grueling training the OSS assigned him to its Morale Operations Branch, to devise propaganda intended to demoralize the enemy. He assisted in the design of pamphlets written in German and Japanese which were to be distributed by secret agents behind the lines to confuse, and undermine the morale of enemy troops and civilians.

Cheek and his colleagues turned out several impressive devices, though he never knew how many, if any, were actually used. Against Hitler's forces they devised a medal for "Friends of the Fuhrer." Wearers received a small red heart-shaped badge which supposedly entitled them to sexual favors from *fräuleins.* For use against the Japanese, they printed spurious Japanese Red Cross leaflets which described in shocking detail medical procedures to be followed in the event of a massive Allied air raid. These graphically illustrated leaflets accidentally foretold the kinds of hideous wounds subsequently suffered by victims of the Hiroshima and Nagasaki atomic bombings.

A month after Germany surrendered on May 7, 1945, Cheek returned joyously to civilian life. As he did after graduating from Yale, he faced a choice of careers. Should he finally become an architect, as he had always planned? Should he look for another museum directorship? Or should he remain in Washington to work with the OSS? Like millions of other young men, Cheek pondered his alternatives.

His best opportunity, he finally decided, was to join the staff of *Architectural Forum,* the handsome magazine published by *Time* and *Life's* Henry Luce. Before he had gone off to war, Cheek had been approached while at the Baltimore Museum by Howard Myers, *Architectural Forum's* publisher, and had been offered a job on the magazine's staff at the war's conclusion. In June of 1945 Leslie accepted the post of associate editor.

CAMOUFLAGE

FIGURE 1.—Men working on P-43 under concealment. Flat-top is supplemented by palm leaves over star and blankets over cockpit windshield and canopy.

CAPT. M. CUTLER

This cover for a technical manual shows the proper way aircraft were to be hidden from enemy detection.

To Engineer Cheek III from
one who knows
Saul STEINBERG
ENGINEER

While in the O.S.S., Cheek met Saul Steinberg, already recognized as one of America's most talented cartoonists. Steinberg made this charming drawing of a locomotive for the Cheeks' eldest son, Leslie III.

At *Architectural Forum* the new editor worked in the Luce publications' offices in the Empire State Building. His role was to research and write feature articles on important architectural developments, like the new campus for the University of Oklahoma, or the new LaGuardia Airport. One of his projects was a three-part study entitled "Houses U.S.A.," a survey of domestic architecture from colonial times to the present. The job brought him into contact with such professionals as Wallace Harrison, Philip Johnson, and Frank Lloyd Wright, whom he interviewed before preparing a cover story on the new Guggenheim Museum.

Hardly had he settled into his new routine at the *Forum's* offices when he heard a tremendous crash and felt the building sway. The relative calm of a Saturday morning in Manhattan was shattered when, on July 28, 1945, a B-25 bomber had slammed into the Empire State Building at 225 m.p.h. Punching a hole nearly 20 feet square between the 78th and 79th floors, the aircraft left thirteen people dead, including the three crew members. One engine plowed through the width of the building, while another plummeted down an elevator shaft.

Fleeing the vacated *Forum* offices, Cheek walked to the Yale Club, where he was besieged by friends at the bar who bought him drinks to hear his version of the crash. The bizarre incident led to new federal regulations governing aircraft movements and mandating skyscraper markings to prevent similar incidents in the future.

In the autumn of 1945, Mary Tyler and the boys moved up from Lake Lure and joined Leslie in a large apartment at 1035 Fifth Avenue, where the family was to live for the next three years. Soon afterward, Mary Tyler returned to Richmond, where their third son, Richard Warfield Cheek was born in October, 1945.

Though the Fifth Avenue apartment was luxurious and the Cheeks had good domestics, they found it hard to rear three lively boys there. Life in Manhattan was not easy.

One of the boys had his sled stolen in Central Park. Leslie did not relish commuting to work by subway. Both Leslie and Mary Tyler missed the quiet and order of their earlier homes.

Though Howard Myers had led Cheek to believe he would serve as a sort of deputy publisher of *Architectural Forum,* the job did not develop that way. However, Cheek swallowed his disappointment for the moment and renewed his ties with the creative world through his work as a member of the Architectural League, the American Society of Interior Design and the Yale Club. He enjoyed his contacts with architects in a time of spectacular post-war expansion in the profession, but he wanted greater latitude in his work.

The Cheeks were saddened in February 1946 by the death of Leslie's mother. Though she had been ailing for several years, Mabel Cheek had made the arduous trip to New York to see and hold her new grandson Richard. For a number of years she had lived on at Cheekwood after her husband's death in 1935, until increasing infirmity forced her to move into a Nashville apartment. To the end, Mabel kept scrapbooks of her children, following Leslie's career with enthusiastic interest.

Mabel Cheek's death added further to her son's inheritance from the family's grocery and coffee fortune, making him fully independent financially. From 1946 onward, he could work at whatever interested him or even quit work entirely and devote himself to travel and art collecting. However, Leslie wisely realized that his interests and temperament would allow him to enjoy life the most only while working full time in the arts or in architecture.

Even though the Time-Life Corporation had given him the task of designing the interiors for some of its executive offices at Springdale, Connecticut, Cheek's discontent with his *Forum* job by 1946 was irretrievable. When Elizabeth Gordon, editor-in-chief of *House Beautiful* magazine offered him a job, he immediately accepted. Moving to new offices only a few blocks away in Manhattan, Cheek

faced his new duties with enthusiasm. His chief responsibility was to develop articles and photographs about important and interesting new houses. He worked closely with Mrs. Gordon, whom he had known since his days in Baltimore. Cheek admired Mrs. Gordon's professionalism, her wide knowledge and her editorial flair.

Looking back later on his New York years, Cheek concluded that he had learned much about magazines, newspapers and photography that he later put to use in his museum career. "There are many similarities in running a magazine and a museum," he said. "You try to give the public a stimulating view of a subject, imaginatively conceived and presented in a readily understandable way." He also learned the importance of print, radio and television in reaching the public.

In 1947 he was appointed by the president of Yale to the newly-formed Yale Council, to serve with his old employer Henry Luce, along with such other notables as publisher John Hay "Jock" Whitney and financier Robert Lehman. On the council Cheek headed a committee, with members Eero Saarinen and Josef Albers, seeking to upgrade Yale's fine arts curriculum. Though the group made many suggestions, few were actually implemented. Cheek continued to serve on the council until 1954, when his term ended.

Despite the challenges of New York life and the pleasure of working with Elizabeth Gordon, Cheek was restless. The optimism which had marked his career thus far seemed to have deserted him. He felt he was going nowhere. He enrolled in night classes in fine arts at Columbia University, and took an agricultural correspondence course through Cornell at Ithaca. He even contacted the recently created Central Intelligence Agency, successor to the OSS, offering his services as an espionage agent.

Cheek was increasingly aware of the noise of Manhattan. He wrote a friend in 1948 that traffic "is particularly bad since 85th Street [which adjoined the Cheek apartment] is a crosstown artery, full of buses and trucks at all

Cheek was an associate editor with *Architectural Forum,* a Henry Luce publication, from 1945 to 1947.

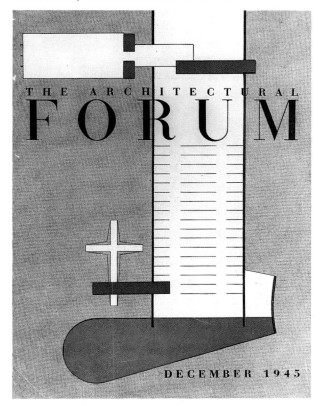

Elizabeth Gordon, editor of *House Beautiful,* hired Cheek in 1947 to work for the magazine, but the job lacked sufficient challenge. Less than a year later, he was named director of the Virginia Museum of Fine Arts. Reprinted by permission of *House Beautiful,* copyright © June 1947. The Hearst Corporation. All Rights Reserved. Maynard Parker, Photographer.

Between 1947 and 1954, Cheek (standing second from the left) was a member of the Yale Council. He and his colleagues on a sub-committee oversaw planning to improve fine arts instruction at Yale University.

These small wax portraits of Leslie III (left) and Douglas Freeman Cheek (right) were executed by Ethel Frances Mundy in the late 1940s. Raising three young children in a Manhattan apartment proved trying for Leslie and Mary Tyler. The move to Richmond in 1948 was prompted in large part by their desire to find a better place for the children to live and grow.

hours of the day . . . Dirt is usually prevalent in this apartment. The grime of passing traffic gases and the dust of ash and garbage collections are daily deposits which require work to remove and much wear to furnishings. This apartment never gets a ray of sunshine. The sun is cut off from it on all sides by buildings." As he wrote someone else, "Raising children in a mid-town apartment is hell."

Then in April of 1948 an interesting possibility appeared. Cheek received a letter from a Richmonder, Webster Rhoads, Jr., inviting him to lunch during Rhoads' forthcoming visit to New York. Rhoads, who had inherited control of Richmond's Miller & Rhoads department store, was vice-president of the Virginia Museum of Fine Arts. After drinks at the Yale Club, Rhoads told Cheek he was seeking leads for a new director of the museum. Without hesitation Cheek offered himself. Surprised, Rhoads said he would put Cheek's name before museum president, Colonel Henry W. Anderson.

To Mary Tyler, who was in Europe with her sister, Leslie wrote enthusiastically of the new prospect. "If the Virginia people want me, and if the job seems as good up close as it does here," he confided on May 12, 1948, "I shall probably accept, for it has many things I desire—and no job will be perfect. However, if things don't work out, I shall not be disheartened for I have gained a bit by the hard year just over and am beginning to see more clearly myself, my life and what I can best do in the future."

Rhoads arranged for Leslie to travel to Richmond to meet Colonel Anderson, who was the senior partner in the Richmond law firm Hunton, Williams, Anderson, Gay and Moore. Anderson had assumed the museum's presidency in July 1947, succeeding former ambassador Alexander W. Weddell.

Webster Rhoads promptly arranged for Cheek to be interviewed. Leslie carefully prepared his presentation. He wrote to his wife, "I have a feeling that the Board wants a 'regular' museum man, with all the old foolishness of the East—not someone to do a program for Richmond and the South. Well, we'll see . . ."

After an interview with Anderson and Rhoads at the colonel's law offices, the three adjourned to the Anderson house on Franklin Street for a elegant lunch, served by Anderson's English butler. "I gathered, as we parted at 3 P.M., that the job was mine if I wanted it," Cheek wrote his wife exultantly. Before entraining for New York, he taxied to the museum and talked with its out-going director, Thomas C. Colt, who had been on the job since the museum's opening twelve years before.

"Colt took me over the museum, which is about one-fourth the size of Baltimore's—and very poorly arranged in every particular," Leslie wrote Mary Tyler. "It was dirty—not so much from lack of daily care, but from the need of refurbishing, and I was very depressed by all I saw . . . Colt said they had many applications from little directors all over the country, but no really good people, as the salary would not attract anyone to such a truly hard job in what seemed—to the museum profession—an isolated spot."

Despite the low salary offered—$7,500 for the first year—Cheek wanted the job, and he said so in a letter dated May 30. On June 12

Webster Rhoads sent him formal notification of his selection by the board of trustees. Leslie wrote Mary Tyler, still in Europe, that he had been accepted. "The job is one that can be of real service to the state and the South," he declared, "if done for a long while, properly backed. I realize that the backing will be my problem, so I enter the undertaking with few illusions and long determination . . ."

Upon Mary Tyler's return from abroad, she joined Leslie in Richmond, where they decided to purchase the former residence of Dr. and Mrs. Shelton Horsley, in Richmond's suburban Westmoreland Place. But of course the house, built in 1919 to designs by Richmond architect Duncan Lee, would need extensive remodeling to satisfy Leslie's exacting demands.

It was a prelude to the most productive period in Leslie Cheek's life. To the Virginia Museum he would give twenty years of creativity, bringing to Virginia and to the museum world a wealth of new ideas to enhance America's greater enjoyment of the arts. To Cheek, as to Thomas Jefferson, "the pursuit of happiness" seemed a legitimate purpose for one's life, especially if it included the arts.   □

The Virginia Museum of Fine Arts, ca. 1948. The original building, inspired by the architecture of Sir Christopher Wren, was designed by Peebles and Ferguson of Norfolk and opened during the Depression in 1936.

CHAPTER VII

The Virginia Museum
SOWING THE SEEDS 1948-1954

John Barton Payne (1855-1935), by Gari Melchers. In 1930 Payne gave $100,000 to start the Virginia Museum, which would house the fifty paintings he had given the state in 1919 as a memorial to his mother and wife.

Like the Baltimore Museum which Leslie Cheek had reinvigorated from 1939 to 1942, the Virginia Museum of Fine Arts, which he took over in July 1948, was a staid and quiet place—a domain of the privileged few. The museum had been opened to the public in 1936, the nation's first state-supported art museum, largely through the generosity of John Barton Payne.

Payne, a Chicago lawyer who had been born in Virginia in 1855, had given $100,000 to start the museum, along with his collection of fifty oil paintings and 300 prints. Payne's vision was ambitious: he hoped to raise the culture of the American South, which even into the early 20th century remained stagnant in the wake of the Civil War and Reconstruction. H.L. Mencken called it "a drying up of civilization." In his essay, "The Sahara of the Bozart," Mencken had written in 1917:

> In all that gargantuan paradise of the fourth-rate there is not a single picture-gallery worth going into, or a single orchestra capable of playing the nine symphonies of Beethoven, or a single opera house, or a single theatre devoted to decent plays, or a single public monument that is worth looking at, or a single workshop devoted to the making of beautiful things . . . In all these fields the South is an awe-inspiring blank—a brother to Portugal, Serbia, and Albania.

Yet John Barton Payne's efforts for Virginia, noble as they were, had a serious shortcoming. Many of the paintings in his collection, unobserved by his amateur eye, were either of doubtful authenticity or had been so over-painted by inept restorers as to make them unrecognizable. Many of these paintings, attributed to Rubens, Canaletto, Murillo, Poussin and other masters were worthless, and were eventually removed from the museum's collection.

But the Virginia Museum was not completely impoverished. A year before Cheek was named director, it had received an unusual collection of *objets d'art* created for Russia's imperial family, the Romanoffs, by the celebrated jeweler Peter Carl Fabergé. These exquisitely crafted jewels had been assembled by Mrs. John Lee Pratt, who had kept them during her lifetime in her bedroom closet. Upon Lillian Pratt's death, her husband, who had known little of the Fabergé collection, found it stuffed in hat boxes.

Pratt told Cheek his wife had begun buying Fabergé objects from Russian jewelry importer Victor Hammer in New York years earlier. She had bought her first Fabergé egg on credit, after much deliberation, to be delivered to her home in Fredericksburg, wrapped in silk brocade. Hammer in turn had obtained the Fabergé items in a trade with the communist government of Russia, in exchange for pencils which his factory mass-produced for the new Soviet state. After buying her first Fabergé egg, Lillian Pratt continued to buy others from Hammer on his periodic sales trips to see her in Fredericksburg.

Another significant museum holding was the collection of early twentieth century paintings given by T. Catesby Jones, a New York lawyer born in Petersburg, Virginia.

Leslie Cheek was faced with the problem of augmenting the museum's limited permanent collection, as well as improving the institution's image. During his first seven years as director, he would succeed in persuading Virginia collectors to give works of art to the museum, as well as money to purchase others. Equally important, he would enliven the museum with imaginative loan exhibitions, would launch the world's first Artmobile, and would create one of the nation's first art museum theatres.

In the first decade of its existence, the Virginia Museum had not been particularly successful at attracting the participation of collectors. John Walker, former director of the National Gallery of Art, observed in his autobiography that much of a museum's work is in enlisting patrons. Such patronage usually takes two forms: the lending or giving of art objects, and the provision of money. Through his association with the museum's president Colonel Henry W. Anderson, Cheek was introduced to wealthy Virginia families who the two men hoped would take an interest in the fledgling institution. Chief among these were the Arthur Glasgows and the Adolph Williamses.

Arthur Glasgow of Richmond, brother of novelist Ellen Glasgow, had emigrated to Britain and made a fortune in gas engineering. He and his wife, Margaret Branch Glasgow, also of Richmond, owned an art collection. Supposedly, the Glasgow's Palm Beach home contained a 5th century Greek sculpture, paintings and furnishings dating from the Italian Renaissance, and jade carvings from China.

Its principal objects, however, were five beautiful Brussels tapestries depicting the Trojan War. Cheek envisioned these adorning the walls of the museum's central hall. He persuaded the Glasgows to make a long-term loan of these to the museum where they would be dramatically lit in a simulated Medieval Hall with an armored knight on horseback, surrounded by military banners and sculptures from the period.

Adolph D. Williams, a wealthy Richmond tobacconist, indulged his wife's passion for art collecting. Since he and Wilkins Coons Williams had no children and few visitors to their granite townhouse at Richmond's Laurel and Franklin Streets, their few valuable paintings were scarcely known to others. Assisted by the New York dealers Bertram and Clyde Newhouse, the Williamses had assembled a very small collection of mostly French and English portraits.

Clyde Newhouse remembers travelling to Richmond about once a month to show the couple works that he thought would interest them. "After [Mrs. Williams] had seen what I brought, her husband would ask, 'Well, Wilkie, do you want it? Do you want it that badly?' Then she'd say, 'I want it,' and that would be the end of it. She did not care what other people bought or wanted." Mrs. Williams was nevertheless amenable to advice, and Cheek, and his assistant, Muriel Christison, were able to persuade the Williamses to direct their buying to meet the needs of the museum. Included among the loan exhibitions which Cheek arranged was one devoted to the collection of these potential donors.

The new director's efforts eventually yielded a rich harvest. The Glasgows were ultimately to leave a large bequest of money, and the Williamses gave the museum their collection—estimated at the time to be worth over $1 million—which included works by J. M. W. Turner, Lucas Cranach, Joshua Reynolds and Thomas Lawrence. The Williamses also left the museum over $2 million in endowment, perhaps the largest bequest ever made at that time to a Southern art museum.

In Cheek's years the museum's collection soared. In 1950 its endowment was less than $250,000. By 1955 it had grown to more than $4 million. This expansion permitted the museum to extend its holdings in Cheek's directorship. Among the acquisitions in Cheek's opening years at the museum were Edward Hopper's *House at Dusk,* purchased through the John Barton Payne Fund, and Renoir's *Jeunes Filles Regardant un Album* (bought in 1953 for the low price of $47,000), and Guardi's *Piazza San Marco* (purchased the following year for a modest $42,000), both acquired through the Williams Fund.

In 1949 Leslie Cheek wrote to Lady Astor, the first woman to sit in Great Britain's Parliament, to request some of her art collection from Cliveden, the Astor estate on the Thames in Buckinghamshire. After a long and sometimes amusing correspondence, the museum received some of Nancy Astor's 18th century English porcelain. As she wrote Cheek at the time, "My family have been badgering me to give it [the porcelain] to them, but they are not going to get it. It was bought for my beloved Virginia." Lady Astor visited the museum in 1951, after which she

Colonel Henry Watkins Anderson (1870-1954), by Alfred Jonniaux. Anderson served as president of the Virginia Museum from 1947-54, and provided much support to Leslie Cheek during his first six years as director. (Courtesy: Virginia Historical Society, Richmond)

wrote Cheek, "I was perfectly delighted to meet you, and see the good work you are doing. I now know that my china will be safe in your keeping and properly shown . . ."

But the most generous of Cheek's patrons was to be Paul Mellon of Upperville. In June of 1949 Colonel Anderson wrote to Cheek, "I have not been able to get Mr. Mellon to take a very active interest in the museum, although he has made contributions from time to time . . ." Soon Cheek invited the Mellons to Richmond and gave them a guided tour of the museum, mentioning plans for an addition. Mrs. Mellon wrote back, "Paul and I were so impressed by your museum and your own personal enthusiasm and ideas, that I had wanted to write and tell you . . . Your new plans for the building are brilliant." It was the beginning of a long relationship between the Cheeks and Mellons and of Paul Mellon's active involvement in museum affairs. It was to flower in his eventual gift of a large collection of French Impressionist paintings and English sporting paintings and drawings, and funds for a new West Wing in which to display them.

In the early years of his directorship Cheek strove to devise ways to attract greater general interest in the museum. Calling upon his experience in Baltimore he produced a series of unusual loan exhibitions. As he told an interviewer, "We use all the gambits we can to get people to come in, with the hope . . . that the museum will make . . . peoples' lives more beautiful . . . So all of our techniques are sort of 'Gone With the Wind' techniques—you know, where Scarlett O'Hara took down the green velvet drawing room curtains and made herself a stylish gown in which to call on Rhett—well, there is a lot of Scarlett O'Hara in us."

Such gambits required a patient board of trustees, who at first did not quite understand the new director's unorthodox methods. He wanted the Virginia Museum to be an inviting cultural center, not an intimidating "forbidden palace" which dispensed culture to the chosen few. Said William Gaines, who served on the museum staff from 1949 until 1982,

"Leslie Cheek had a vision of what a museum might contribute to a community, whether that would be a nation, a state, a city or a neighborhood. The arts became a way of life, not just one of those things you do sometimes . . ."

Cheek was fortunate to serve under four museum presidents who gave him their full confidence: Henry W. Anderson (1948-54), Webster S. Rhoads, Jr. (1954-57), John Garland Pollard, Jr. (1958-60), and Walter S. Robertson (1960-1967). But the board was persuaded only in part by the endorsement of these men, though their backing helped. They were impressed, instead, by Cheek's performance: increased membership, higher income, greater publicity and a larger endowment.

These results were evident in Cheek's spectacular previews for museum members the night before each exhibition opened. These were black-tie affairs, with receiving lines, and well-served refreshments. Thanks to the tireless efforts of Richmond caterers Benjamin and Frances Lambert, under the direction of Frances Banks, the museum's membership secretary, these receptions and gala dinners were as appetizing as they were elegant.

String music often played as guests, assisted by staff members in evening dress, milled around fountains and flower arrangements. Outside, in front of the museum, lighted signs and flags proclaimed to passersby what was going on inside. The signs were created by John Koenig, a talented Yale designer Cheek brought from San Francisco.

Guy Friddell, who served briefly as public information officer of the museum from 1949 to 1950, recalls Cheek's early years: "In his lust for detail [Cheek] first had to do everything himself to set the standard. It wasn't that he couldn't delegate duties, but there was a sheer lack of manpower in the early days. Invitations and catalogues had to be perfect. They were little works of art . . . triumphs of good taste which caused their readers to say, 'Now here's something special.'"

Museum workers grew accustomed to

seeing their director strolling about the galleries, righting chairs which had been knocked slightly akilter, or clambering up a ladder in shirtsleeves, hammering nails or adjusting a spotlight. Staff members, often joined by volunteers, returned to the museum after work to get everything ready for the preview.

Arriving at their desks the following morning staffers invariably found thank-you notes in Cheek's distinctive scrawl. Richard Velz, then the museum's administrator, said, "Leslie Cheek was a perfectionist . . . He *was* hard to work for, but [his] great genius was an ability to see the importance of team work and team spirit. Without that, your organization just can't get the job done."

All of this hard work had but one aim: "to draw people into that museum," as Friddell put it. A visitor who attended one of the four or five big shows which marked Cheek's early years in office could not help but become more interested in art, and in the goings-on at the increasingly lively museum.

Healy's Sitters, which opened in January of 1950, was Cheek's first sizable show, devoted to the works of George P. A. Healy, the portraitist who painted eleven American presidents from life. As Cheek wrote in the exhibition catalogue, Healy was "America's first international portraitist, [whose] work is at once a visual 'Who's Who' of the 19th century, and a record of the changing taste of that romantic era." Some of the art was already in the museum's possession, since the John Barton Payne collection contained nine Healy works. The Corcoran Gallery, the Newberry Library and the Smithsonian were other lenders.

Guy Friddell recalled the Healy exhibition as one in which Cheek ". . . put together a kind of 'national family album' on the walls and in the catalogue. Lots of time and effort went into the catalogue, which had to be just the right color, and the gold embossed lettering on the cover had to be just right." In typical Cheek fashion, the ambience of the 19th century was re-created through the use of Victorian furniture and graphics in the galleries.

Cheek's second season was highlighted by a controversy some called the "Battle of Richmond," pitting conservative Ross Valentine, a columnist for the *Richmond Times Dispatch*, against modern art. The first shots were fired after the opening of *Calder and Sculpture Today* in October 1949, when Valentine, offended by the *avant garde* display, denounced modern art as communist infiltration. "The important thing in the Red sophistry," he wrote, "is to intrigue the mind while it is still formative, to instill distortions of truth which seem to relieve the intellect from the burden of moral discipline and respect for sound standards in art, statesmanship and ethics." Not surprisingly, this acerbic column provoked letters to the editor which defended the new trends. But Valentine insisted that ". . . those who subscribe to the aberrations . . . in art . . . contribute to the razing of our civlization so that their masters in the Kremlin may build upon its ruins and ashes a sepulchre to our freedoms."

The battle became more heated when the *American Painting* biennial opened at the museum in April of 1950. Valentine denounced it as a collection of "ultra-modern daubs," little more than "grotesqueries, distortions, and downright adulation of morbidity." He was incensed when James Johnson Sweeney, whom Cheek had invited to judge the show, selected Stuart Davis' *Little Giant Still Life* for top honors. He was equally indignant when Cheek persuaded the board of trustees to purchase the canvas (at a cost of $3,400, considered modest by art experts) for the museum's collection. The Valentine-Sweeney face-off made the pages of *Art News*, and the *New York Herald Tribune*.

Valentine's newspaper denunciations continued for the first six years of Cheek's directorship, steadily increasing public interest in the museum. Meanwhile, the museum continued to acquire and display new contemporary art. Acquisitions of the 1950s besides the Stuart Davis work included a Calder mo-

The idea for an exhibition devoted to the works of George P. A. Healy was suggested to Cheek by Elizabeth Binford, wife of artist Julien Binford. The show opened in January, 1950. One of the Healy paintings, *The Peacemakers*, was loaned by the White House.

Stuart Davis, *Little Giant Still Life*. Some Richmonders were shocked when it won top honors at the Virginia Museum's 1950 *American Painting* biennial. Cheek later persuaded the museum's board to buy the controversial painting.

ABOVE AND OPPOSITE PAGE: Cheek's training in theatre design was evident in *Furniture of the Old South* held at the museum in 1952. The exhibition, which took two years to organize, was a scholarly examination of Southern decorative arts.

Habiliments for Heroines exhibited the feminine dress of sixteen literary figures. Esther Waters (top), from the 1894 novel by George Moore, is shown in her bedroom ready to go to her first Derby. Sharlee Weyland (right), from Henry S. Harrison's *Queed* (1911), makes her way down a busy city street, accompanied by her faithful dog, "Behemoth."

bile and a large metal sculpture by Harry Bertoia, entitled *Golden Tree*.

Cheek's flair for recreating an exotic time or place was seen in *Dutch and Flemish Paintings from the Chrysler Collection*. Squares of masonite were painted black and white, and temporarily placed over the gallery floor to imitate the polished marble flooring of medieval Holland, which often appeared in the works of Rembrandt, Hals and Vermeer. Heavy carved tables, covered with Oriental rugs were borrowed from Richmond collectors. Because Dutch artists were adept at painting sunlight in their canvases, Cheek recreated its effects with pale yellow spotlights. It was as if museum-goers were walking through the paintings themselves.

Other imaginative techniques were used in January of 1952 when *Furniture of the Old South, 1640-1820* opened. Aware of the need for new support for the museum, Cheek staged a reception for the Governor and members of the General Assembly. The show, two years in the making, was the brainchild of Alice Winchester, editor of *The Magazine Antiques*, who helped Cheek organize this first comprehensive survey of Southern decorative arts. Included were furnishings from nine states. As part of the exhibition, one gallery was transformed into a Southern drawing room and was warmed by a lifelike hearth fire. To add a homey touch, Cheek advertised for a stuffed cat to lie near the fireplace. He received many and he accepted them all, changing the cat each day of the exhibit.

Moving from decorative arts to fashion, the museum in 1952 offered *Habiliments for Heroines*, an examination of styles of dress.

The exhibit displayed a succession of sixteen literary heroines, dressed as described by novelists of the past. As a preliminary, Junior League volunteers read works by Oliver Goldsmith, Henry James, George Meredith, Louisa May Alcott, Charles Dickens, and others for passages describing feminine dress. Help in locating the costumes to match the texts was provided by the Costume Institute of the Metropolitan Museum. Costumes were loaned by Richmond's Valentine Museum, the Museum of the City of New York and Richmond citizens.

The elegance of Hanoverian England was illustrated by a scene from Tobias Smollett's 1748 novel, *Roderick Random*. Comely Narcissa Topehall, "dressed in a blue damask sacque . . . her beautiful hair in ringlets . . . aglow with modesty and love," was presented as she entered a Georgian drawing room to be married to the novel's hero. The museum asked fashion designer Pauline Trigere to provide a cocktail dress for Elsi Metellus, a character from Josephine Pinckney's *My Son and Foe*, published in 1952. Mannequins had to be specially made, since the dresses of past centuries were so small they could not fit contemporary figures.

Museum-goers could see how pioneer photographers worked in the 1860s and '70s through the recreated photographic studio of *Southern Exposures*, which opened in November 1952. Visitors posed for their likeness while a museum staff member held aloft his flash pan, and directed the sitter from behind his draped camera, mounted on a tripod. The antique camera actually concealed a modern Polaroid, providing an instant photograph for each sitter. Afterwards, visitors viewed an exhibition of recently-discovered Civil War photographs, most of them the work of George Smith Cook and his son, Huestis Cook, pioneer Southern photographers.

Probably the most far-reaching of Cheek's exhibitions in his early years was *Design in Scandinavia* in 1954. Selection of the Virginia Museum to coordinate the international show was a tribute to Leslie Cheek, who

A recreated 19th century photographer's studio was the centerpiece of *Southern Exposures*. The exhibition, held in 1952, featured the work by Civil War photographers George and Huestis Cook. The camera at right concealed a modern Polaroid camera used to take souvenir pictures of museum visitors.

OPPOSITE PAGE: The installation for *Design in Scandinavia*, designed by Denmark's Erik Herlow, folded up into containers for ease of transportation. The Virginia Museum was selected in 1954 to coordinate the American tour of the internationally-acclaimed exhibition devoted to the best designed objects for the home from Norway, Denmark, Sweden and Finland.

had established himself by this time as a highly innovative museum administrator. Art achieved what diplomacy alone had not, bringing Norway, Denmark, Sweden and Finland together for a splendid exhibition. After its Richmond premiere, it toured other museums.

The exhibition consisted of over 700 objects: glass, silver, fabrics and furniture. They were the best designed objects from Scandinavian countries for home use. As Cheek wrote in the catalogue: "Every human is interested in objects for his home. He wants them to be as efficient and pleasing as possible, for he must use them daily throughout his life. In the world today there is no group of people who have designed better objects for the home than the Scandinavians." The installation, including cases and lighting, was designed by Erik Herlow, a Danish architect who won a competition among Scandinavians for the plan.

President Eisenhower, the kings of Norway, Sweden and Denmark, and the president of Finland served as patrons for the show. The night before the opening was marked by a colorful international dinner served at Richmond's Commonwealth Club, with the ambassador from each Scandinavian country attending.

While the public was enjoying his wide variety of exhibitions, Cheek was originating other programs. One was the world's first Artmobile. From the beginning, he had been determined to make the museum serve all Virginians whose taxes helped support it. When he arrived in 1948, he found that museum extension services consisted of sending boxes of do-it-yourself art exhibits to Virginia libraries, schools and colleges. Few communities requested the exhibits, which were usually ill-displayed and poorly protected. In 1950 he began to consider the possibilities of a self-contained art gallery on wheels. He was impressed by the success of recently-introduced Bookmobiles, which took books to rural areas from city libraries.

Cheek decided that a trailer pulled by a

113

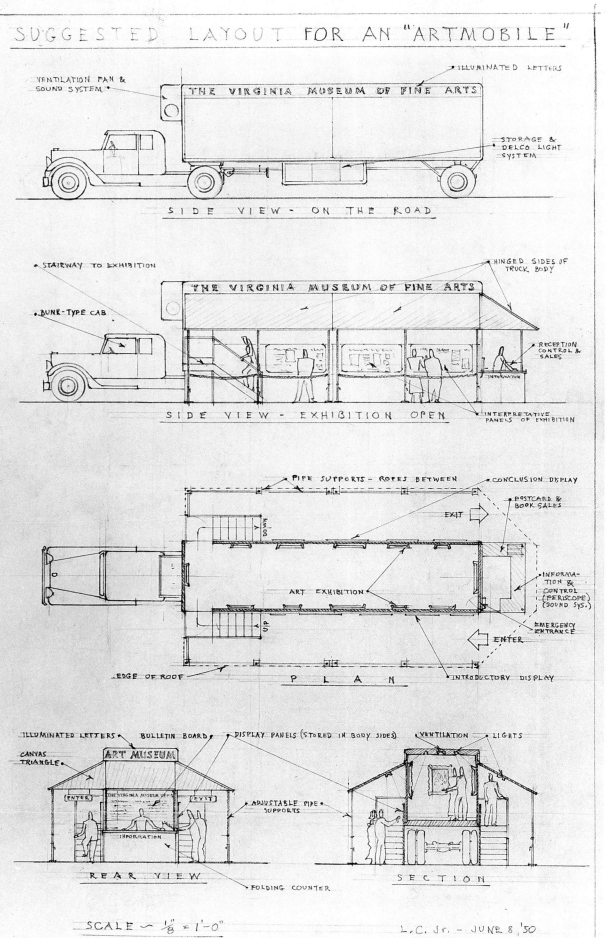

SUGGESTED LAYOUT FOR AN "ARTMOBILE"

VENTILATION FAN & SOUND SYSTEM

ILLUMINATED LETTERS

THE VIRGINIA MUSEUM OF FINE ARTS

STORAGE & DELCO LIGHT SYSTEM

SIDE VIEW - ON THE ROAD

STAIRWAY TO EXHIBITION

HINGED SIDES OF TRUCK BODY

THE VIRGINIA MUSEUM OF FINE ARTS

BUNK-TYPE CAB

RECEPTION CONTROL & SALES

SIDE VIEW - EXHIBITION OPEN

INTERPRETATIVE PANELS OF EXHIBITION

PIPE SUPPORTS - ROPES BETWEEN

CONCLUSION DISPLAY

POSTCARD & BOOK SALES

EXIT

ART EXHIBITION

INFORMATION & CONTROL (PERISCOPE) (SOUND SYS.)

EMERGENCY ENTRANCE

ENTER

EDGE OF ROOF

PLAN

INTRODUCTORY DISPLAY

ILLUMINATED LETTERS   BULLETIN BOARD   DISPLAY PANELS (STORED IN BODY SIDES)   VENTILATION   LIGHTS

CANVAS TRIANGLE

ART MUSEUM

ENTER   THE VIRGINIA MUSEUM OF...   EXIT

INFORMATION

ADJUSTABLE PIPE SUPPORTS

REAR VIEW

FOLDING COUNTER

SECTION

SCALE ~ 1/8" = 1'-0"

L. C. Jr. - JUNE 8, '50

tractor would work best, accordingly designing a special 34-foot trailer—the largest then permitted by law on Virginia's highways. Cheek's new Artmobile expanded to 51 feet in length and 22 feet in width when its side panels were unfolded. He specified that the trailer be left unpainted, its gleaming aluminum decorated with a blue band and white lettering—"Art Museum" at the front and back, and "The Virginia Museum of Fine Arts" on the sides. The tractor was also painted blue.

The trailer's side panels were hinged so they could be lifted to provide shelter for those waiting to enter. It carried information on placards describing the exhibition inside. Detachable stairs, carried beneath the trailer, were placed at the Artmobile's two doorways. Art objects were firmly attached to the walls and lit with spotlights. The first Artmobile had to be connected to a 220 volt outlet wherever it parked to provide power for its lighting, sound, security alarm and air-conditioning systems. But later Artmobiles—there would be three larger versions added during Cheek's tenure—were equipped with their own generators on the tractor units.

The first Artmobile took to Virginia's roads in 1953, a gift from Miller and Rhoads department stores. The tractor was donated by John Lee Pratt of Fredericksburg, long a generous patron and trustee of the museum. The Virginia Federation of Women's Clubs contributed $10,000 for first year operating expenses. The traveling museum was dedicated on October 13, 1953, at Maury Elementary School in Fredericksburg. There ex-Governor William M. Tuck, in whose administration the project had begun, presented the achievement to his successor, Governor John S. Battle.

Time magazine described the event in its issue of October 19: "A big 45-foot aluminum trailer truck rumbled into Fredericksburg, Va., one day this week and parked near an elementary school. Outside it looked like any ordinary truck, but inside it was unusual; it contained a small, well-stocked art gallery.

OPPOSITE PAGE: Leslie Cheek's pencil drawing dated June, 1950, of the world's first Artmobile. Cheek was inspired to create a gallery-on-wheels by Virginia's highly successful Bookmobile program. **ABOVE:** Artmobile I was instrumental in carrying out the museum's purpose to bring art to the people of the Commonwealth. During its first two years, over 60,000 Virginians visited the mobile art gallery. As a member of President Eisenhower's People-to-People Program, Cheek wanted Artmobiles to be employed on a global scale, but his idea was judged impractical.

RIGHT: October 13, 1953 dedication ceremonies for Artmobile I in Fredericksburg. (Left to right) Edwin Hyde, Mrs. Waverly Cousins, Walter P. Chrysler, Jr., Leslie Cheek, Mrs. H. Stanley Bailey and Governor John Battle.

LEFT: The museum later added three more Artmobiles. Among the exhibitions which toured Virginia communities in them were (top) *Conversation Pieces*, with paintings from 18th century England in the collection of Mr. and Mrs. Paul Mellon. Rich red walls set off paintings (bottom) from the Maxim Karolik Collection in *American Sampler: Painting, 1815-1865*. Installations in the Artmobiles were designed with the same care and precision as were those which appeared in the museum itself.

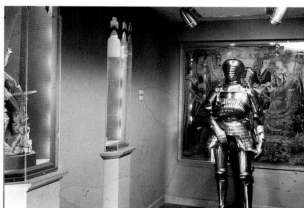

ABOVE: *Medieval Treasures* included this suit of armor, tapestries, and statuary in glass-covered niches set into the walls of the Artmobile.

The truck was Virginia's new 'Artmobile,' the U.S.'s first art gallery on wheels. Its purpose: to bring art to people who ordinarily never set foot inside a museum." *Newsweek* also carried a story and color photographs of the Artmobile's interior and exterior. The first show was *The Little Dutch Masters,* from the collection of Walter P. Chrysler, Jr., featuring sixteen paintings by such masters as Bosch, van de Velde, van Ruysdael and ter Borch.

Five years after the Artmobile's inauguration, John Walker, then the director of the National Gallery of Art in Washington wrote, "In the whole field of museum education, the Artmobile seems to me the most significant development of the last twenty years." This gallery on wheels truly fulfilled the museum's legislative mandate to "promote throughout the Commonwealth education in the realm of art . . . ," and its drivers served as goodwill ambassadors, spreading the name, activities and promise of the Virginia Museum of Fine Arts.

A few months after the Cheeks moved to Richmond their fourth child was born in June of 1949. She was Elizabeth Tyler Cheek. Her older brothers were kept busy at school and at home, for their father gave them chores to be done each week, just as his parents had given him in Nashville. One was to water the ivy which Cheek had planted around a six-foot masonry wall he had built around his house and gardens. It was one of the many improvements Cheek was to make to the place. In 1955, the original front steps were replaced with limestone ones in Greek Revival manner. At the same time the front porch colonnade and the windows above it were changed, for Cheek felt the originals were "too 1919." Part of the front lawn was made into a parking area for five automobiles, and other parking was added adjacent to the vegetable garden. Lighting was provided by large Georgian-style pier lanterns.

The family continued to summer at Faraway Farm. Often, Mary Tyler and the children would go after school had ended in June while Leslie remained at work at the museum.

Richard, Douglas and Leslie III wearing special hats their father made for July 4, 1951, celebrations at Lake Lure. The Cheeks entertained at holiday cook-outs at Faraway Farm to which townspeople were invited.

Occasionally, when his schedule permitted, he would make the nine hour drive to Lake Lure for weekend visits. There he organized family festivities such as he had enjoyed in childhood. The high point was the July 4 celebration in which family and guests dressed as pirates, military heroes and other characters. The procession paraded to the boathouse, where neighbors assembled for a picnic and fireworks.

In 1951 *House Beautiful* published an elaborate color article about Faraway Farm, describing it as a place "utterly free of prescribed dogma." It added: "It is unpretentious to the point of plainness. Yet it is truly luxurious—in the American sense that its first rule is the comfort of the people who live there."

But the distant farm was also becoming a burden. While it grew fruits, vegetables, chickens and dairy products for the family, it was not profitable. Accordingly, Cheek in 1952 wrote to Lee Powers in Lake Lure that "our family is in no financial condition to operate two houses. Having a farm does necessitate the constant spending of money and since our supply of that important ingredient is decreasing rather than increasing, we literally cannot afford to fool around with Faraway much longer."

Cheek was facing the costs of sending the boys away to preparatory schools, and he also wanted to make additions to the Richmond house. Besides, the Internal Revenue Service had notified him that since the farm had not made profits, he could no longer deduct its expenses on his tax returns.

Faraway Farm was sold in 1955 to a Florida businessman. The family was reluctant to part with it, for they loved the house and its tranquil setting. "All of us are still pretty numb at the truly severe shock of pulling our roots out of that handsome countryside. . . ," Cheek wrote Lee Powers. However, the appeal of rural life never faded from Cheek's memory, and ten years later he would plan another country retreat.

After his first six years at the museum, Leslie Cheek could look back on many achievements: building an endowment for art purchases, producing an amazing variety of loan exhibitions and creating the Artmobile. He invited important figures from the arts to lecture at the museum, including Edward Steichen, Naum Gabo, Victor Hammer, Robert Osborn and Philip Johnson. Listed among the earliest guest speakers was John Canaday, who visited the museum in December, 1948. At that time Canaday was a professor of art history at the University of Virginia. A friend of Cheek, he later became art critic for the *New York Times.*

Despite these accomplishments Cheek was not ready to sit still. He was forever thinking of the museum as a cultural center to serve and delight a wide audience. A new wing, which was already being discussed when he arrived, gave him a chance to turn his thoughts into further action. ☐

Cheek designed these kiosks to display the Lillian Thomas Pratt Collection of Russian Imperial Jewels. To the delight of museum-goers the rare and precious objects by Peter Carl Fabergé glowed mysteriously against red velvet in the dimly lit entrance hall. The kiosks were unveiled to the public in December, 1954.

CHAPTER VIII

The Virginia Museum
GROWTH 1954-1960

At the top level of the $2.2 million North Wing, completed in 1954-55, was the Mediterranean Court. Galleries with movable walls and the unique Lusklite system were in rooms adjacent to this atrium. Receptions for museum previews were often held in this classically-inspired court. The North Wing met Cheek's objectives of tasteful and flexible display areas for the museum's growing collections. On floors below the Mediterranean Court were the Museum Theatre and Members' Room, both opened in 1955.

On October 29, 1954, the North Wing was formally dedicated. In the receiving line at the reception were (left to right) Mrs. Walter S. Robertson, former Governor and Mrs. William M. Tuck, Governor Thomas B. Stanley (Mrs. Stanley, in the white gown, is almost totally obscured), and Mr. and Mrs. Webster Rhoads. Behind are two of the five 17th century Flemish tapestries, *The Tale of Troy*, from the Glasgow Collection.

The evening of October 29, 1954, was a sparkling one at the Virginia Museum. Over 1,600 guests turned out in formal dress for the opening of the new North Wing. The reception chiefly honored Governor and Mrs. Thomas B. Stanley. Two former governors, John S. Battle and William M. Tuck, were present and spoke over the live radio broadcast from the museum.

The 1954 wing began a series of Virginia Museum expansions that was to continue at a steady pace through the 1980s. They were made necessary by the museum's wide popularity and the resultant growth of its collections.

The 1954 opening climaxed a series of dedicatory events. In September the museum had unveiled Carl Milles' *Small Triton Fountain* on its Boulevard terrace, the gift of Mrs. George Baker of New York. A month later Mayor Thomas Pinckney Bryan had presided to activate the new Woodson P. Waddy fountains flanking the Boulevard entrance. Waddy, a Richmond stationer, had bequeathed a large sum for outdoor fountains like those at Washington's National Gallery. However, Cheek deemed them out of scale for the smaller Virginia Museum and persuaded the Waddy family to accept an alternative design, which he developed with Eggers and Higgins, New York architects.

The North Wing and its beautiful theatre doubled the museum's original size. After long efforts by Cheek to find a suitable design and funding, it was urgently needed. Almost from the beginning in 1936, the museum's facilities had proved inadequate. The original plans by Peebles and Ferguson, the Norfolk firm that designed the original museum, had envisioned wings to be added to its north and south ends, in the same Christopher Wren style as the original. The need for this space was evident to the trustees as early as 1940. When Cheek took over in 1948, the Commonwealth had just appropriated funds for an addition. The new director then immediately began to plan a North Wing.

Cheek's concept grew from his populist view of what an ideal state-supported art museum should be. He wrote in *Theatre Arts* magazine in 1951 that "In addition to painting and the other graphic arts, the Virginia Museum plans to use the dynamic arts of theatre, both ancient and modern, to help expand and enrich the cultural life of the people of the entire state . . . Live actors saying words and singing songs of another era, near a display of examples of painting, sculpture and architecture from that era, together make for a deeper comprehension of historic art."

At the Baltimore Museum Cheek had experimentally added a theatre, and he found it had enriched visitors' experience. Now he proposed that Virginia should add a Museum Theatre for the dramatic arts, including film and television.

The proposed wing would also give opportunity to add galleries that were flexible and equipped with variable lighting. Both the Virginia and Baltimore museums, as originally built, had large exhibition halls with thick walls, ill-adapted to new configurations. Cheek had surmounted this in Baltimore by erecting temporary partitions which cut large rooms into smaller spaces, providing generous wall space to display art advantageously. In Richmond Cheek now planned a wing with the built-in flexibility of movable walls and controlled lighting.

The Virginia Museum before Cheek had relied on overhead skylights and electrical fixtures which diffused cold white light through the galleries. Cheek doggedly created a more versatile and theatrical lighting apparatus, based on his experiences since his Yale years. He proposed to use light creatively, in order to define and dramatize art. With the help of Carroll B. Lusk, the Yale-trained lighting technician on the museum staff, he devised a scheme to focus one beam of uniform intensity on each art object. Cheek justified his technique with the explanation that the typical

The North Wing (right) followed the Wren-inspired style of the original building. The Woodson P. Waddy Fountains (foreground) were added to the Boulevard facade, along with the distinctive flagpoles in 1954.

ABOVE RIGHT: The library in the North Wing was added to house the museum's growing collection of art books and periodicals. In 1970 a new library was opened in the South Wing, and this room was converted to a sales area for the Council Shop. The portrait is of John Barton Payne, by Gari Melchers. **RIGHT:** The Members' Room, completed in 1955, was furnished by Florence Knoll with designs by Eames, Saarinen and Mies. In this area museum members met before entering the Refreshment Room through the door at right. Note the Alexander Calder mobile, and the Members' Garden beyond the windows. The statue is *Pandora* by Chauncey B. Ives (1810-1894).

121

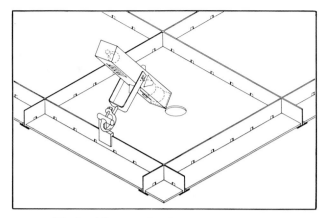

ABOVE: The Lusklite permitted a single high-intensity beam to be directed downward onto art objects through small holes cut in ceiling panels. **BELOW:** Flexible walls made it easier to assemble gallery spaces of varying dimensions. (Drawing by Robert W. Stewart)

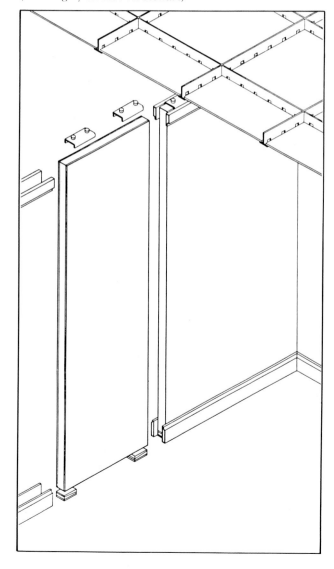

A museum workman is shown adjusting a Lusklite in a North Wing gallery. Cheek used Lusklites to focus visitors' attention on the art objects displayed.

museum-goer was interested in art, not the gallery in the background.

Delay in building the North Wing unfortunately occurred. Structural steel was scarce in the early 1950s because of the Korean War, and warships and planes had prior claim on the nation's resources. However, the National Production Authority in 1952 finally granted the museum an exemption from wartime restrictions, in recognition of its pressing need for more space. Even so, the museum could not locate suitable steel until 1953.

The North Wing was finally built, providing three useful levels. On the topmost was the beautiful Mediterranean Court, a classic atrium with a pool and fountain surrounded by twelve massive Doric columns. Around the court were galleries for exhibitions, in each of which were movable walls as well as an audio system. Above the ceilings was space for technicians to install Lusklites for each exhibition. An opening could readily be made in the quarter-inch-thick ceiling panels to permit a light beam to enhance an art object below. General gallery illumination was by floodlights above translucent ceiling panels.

The middle floor of the $2.2 million North Wing was for offices, a workshop, a photographic laboratory, art storage and packing rooms, and a reception area. A library was provided for the growing book and slide collection, which was becoming one of the best in the South.

The lower level of the North Wing was the most difficult to build and the most sensational. It housed the technically advanced Museum Theatre, which was scheduled for completion a year after the rest of the wing, plus the handsome new Members' Suite.

The first show in the North Wing galleries was *Masterpieces of Chinese Art*, the largest exhibition of Chinese art ever shown in the South to that date. It opened in November 1954, unveiling a sumptuous collection of carved jades, some from as early as 500 BC, along with ritual bronzes, paintings, ceramics and carved gems. Museum-goers viewed well-preserved embroideries and silks worn by

Masterpieces of Chinese Art was the first exhibition staged in the North Wing's loan gallery. These specially-built manne- quins displayed silks and embroideries worn by Chinese aristocrats from 200 B.C. to 1800 A.D.

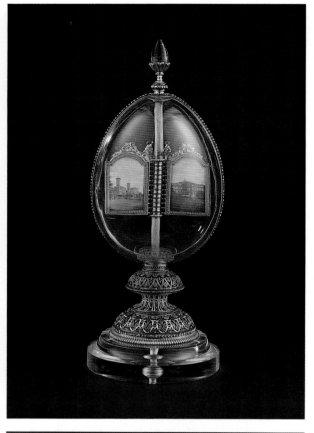

ABOVE: This close-up view shows the arrangement of several Fabergé objects in one of the specially-built kiosks. **ABOVE RIGHT:** This Imperial Easter egg was presented to Czarina Alexandra Feodorovna by Nicholas II in 1896. The rock crystal globe is topped with a Siberian cabochon emerald. The *champlevé* enamel and gold base is worked with Russian and German monograms of the Czarina, set with diamonds. The egg contains miniatures of various royal residences. **RIGHT:** The Fabergé poppy has stamens of gold set with sapphires and centers set with topaz. The delicate blossom and bud are of peach-toned chalcedony. Its agate tub has diamond rivets fastening the two gold hoops.

Chinese nobles from 200 years before Christ until 1800 years after, exhibited on mannequins specially made for the display.

Soon thereafter *Native Art of the Northwest Pacific Coast* opened in the new loan gallery. To give the visitor a sense of being in the forests of British Columbia, Cheek scented the galleries with pine. He had found a men's cologne with that fragrance and hid open bottles in the gallery. To his dismay, the ventillating system sometimes wafted the smell into the nearby Medieval Hall, and French and Italian galleries.

In December 1954, 600 people attended a special showing of the museum's Fabergé jewelry collection. Until this event, the Fabergé treasures had been kept in a bank vault except for an annual four-day showing at Easter. The collection was made up of tiny jeweled eggs, picture frames, flowers, boxes and figurines which the jeweler Peter Carl Fabergé had made for Russia's last Czar, Nicholas II.

Impressed by the crowds attracted by the Fabergé jewels, Cheek had designed three permanent kiosks in which to show them. Each kiosk was decorated with heraldic symbols of imperial Russia and topped by the Romanoffs' double eagle. The objects stood out against a red velvet background in the sombre Entrance Hall, dimly lit by Cheek's spectacular installation of a ten-foot branching chandelier, acquired from French and Company, New York antiquarians.

Carlisle Humelsine, a museum trustee and at that time president of the Colonial Williamsburg Foundation, was especially pleased with public response to the North Wing. He wrote Cheek that the museum "certainly offers a fine example of what you can achieve by a judicious mixing of careful planning, imagination, hard work, and superb taste . . . It illustrates the fact that if you have sufficient quality, the quantity problem will take care of itself."

Before the North Wing's first season had ended, Cheek began planning the most ambitious exhibition in the museum's history. He wanted to show the world how Hollywood made a feature motion picture. To gauge public response he polled the directors of two dozen other museums and asked if they would be interested in such an exhibition. About twenty said yes.

Cheek then called his friend Frank McCarthy, a Richmond-born executive with 20th Century Fox. McCarthy agreed to approach Samuel Goldwyn and suggest that one of his productions be the exhibition's subject. Cheek was encouraged to go to Hollywood and try to persuade the legendary producer, but Goldwyn declined. Cheek then went to Paramount, where McCarthy introduced him to Cecil B. DeMille and Charlton Heston on the set for *The Ten Commandments*.

At first DeMille was enthusiastic about Cheek's plan. A few weeks later, Cheek sent museum designer John Koenig to Hollywood with a scenario of the exhibition for DeMille to study. To the museum's annoyance, DeMille kept Koenig waiting six weeks in Hollywood while the scenario was passed from one office to another. Paramount finally said no, blaming high costs. Cheek was crestfallen, but he kept the idea in mind for later implementation.

Meanwhile, the director prepared to open the Members' Suite in September 1955, on the lower level of the North Wing. It was composed of a Members' Room, Refreshment Room and Members' Garden. In the first, members and their guests could gather before visiting the galleries, the theatre, or the adjoining Refreshment Room. The suite was decorated and furnished by Florence Knoll, well-known New York designer. The chairs had been designed by Eero Saarinen and Mies van de Rohe, while the rug was by V'Soske. Paintings and accessories were by Picasso, Dufy and Braque, while an Alexander Calder mobile hung from the ceiling.

Waitresses in yellow and white uniforms served members, taking orders from menus of matching hues. Cheek commissioned a lively painting for a decorative screen to divide the Refreshment Room from the kitchen.

In 1955 Cheek journeyed to a Hollywood soundstage to enlist the cooperation of director Cecil B. De Mille (left) for a Virginia Museum exhibition devoted to movie making. Actor Charlton Heston listens in on the conversation. The film exhibition proved too expensive to carry out and the idea was shelved.

The family at Cheekwood in 1956: Douglas, Leslie, Jr., Mary Tyler, Richard and Leslie III. Daughter Elizabeth Tyler Cheek is not in this photograph.

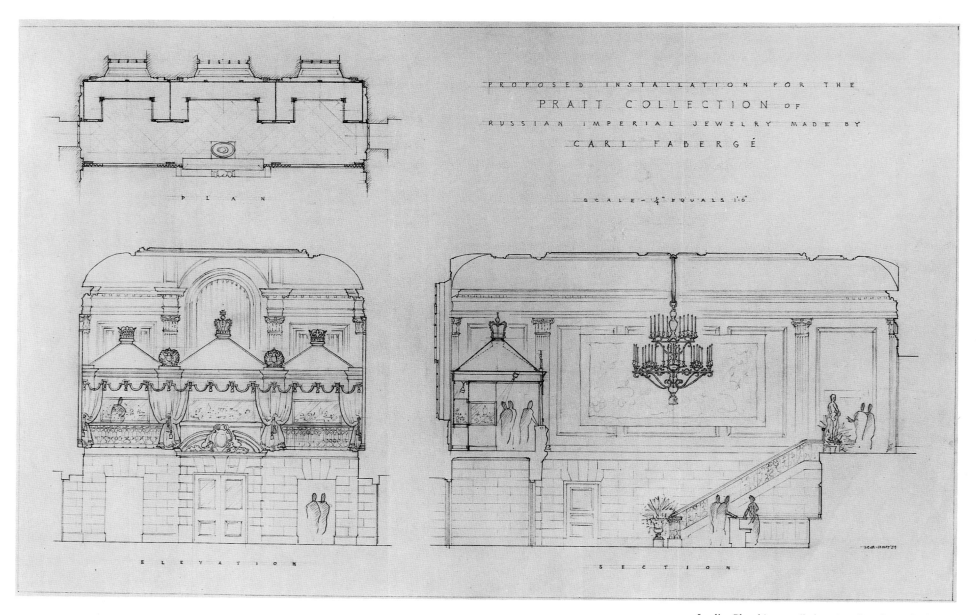

PROPOSED INSTALLATION FOR THE
PRATT COLLECTION OF
RUSSIAN IMPERIAL JEWELRY MADE BY
CARL FABERGÉ

SCALE - ¼" EQUALS 1'-0"

PLAN

ELEVATION

SECTION

ABOVE: Leslie Cheek's pencil drawing for the refurbished entrance hall, chandelier and Fabergé kiosks. **RIGHT:** The museum's drab entrance hall (top) as it appeared before the 1954 renovations. Construction workers (bottom) prepare to hoist into place the ten-foot wide chandelier made by French and Company of New York. Unfinished Fabergé kiosks are on the balcony. The 18th century Gobelins tapestry, *The Triumph of Hercules,* was the gift of Mrs. Alfred I. duPont. **FAR RIGHT:** This photograph of the renovated entrance hall was taken from the balcony on which the Fabergé kiosks were installed. A desk doubling as an information and sales area was at the base of the staircase. Through the doorway can be seen the central Medieval Hall, site of many museum receptions and dinners. In the summer of 1985 this entrance hall was completely altered: the immense chandelier was removed, the Fabergé display was taken out and windows once blocked by the kiosks were reopened to bright sunlight.

127

LEFT: The elegantly furnished Virginia Museum Members' Room. **LEFT BELOW:** The Refreshment Room looked out into the Members' Garden, and provided a quiet haven for diners.

ABOVE: At first the Museum Council's gift shop, which opened for business in 1962, consisted of these mobile carts. Cheek designed them to be pushed throughout the galleries. In 1976 the shop moved to larger quarters in what was once the North Wing library.

This colorful screen by Richard Q. Yardley of the *Baltimore Sun* was used at the Refreshment Room serving window to hide the kitchen from the view of diners. Entitled *Here's*

How it depicts famous painters, sculptors, architects, dancers and composers from the past admiring the *avant garde* works of their modern-day counterparts.

Two trustees, Mrs. John Bocock of Richmond and Admiral Lewis Strauss of Culpeper, provided $1,500 with which Cheek commissioned a cartoon-style depiction of celebrated creators from the worlds of painting, dance, sculpture, music, drama and architecture.

At first Cheek hoped Julien Binford, who taught at Mary Washington College, would execute it. When Binford was unable to do so, Cheek asked Richard Q. Yardley, veteran *Baltimore Sun* cartoonist, to do the job. Yardley, who had known Cheek in Baltimore, produced a whimsical depiction that struck the right convivial note. The popular work, titled *Here's How*, brightened the Refreshment Room for many years.

The Members' Suite had floor-to-ceiling windows and sliding glass doors opening into the Members' Garden. The latter was landscaped by Alfred Geiffert of New York, who had previously planned the museum's grounds and landscaped the National Gallery in Washington. Members could sit in the garden beside a pool in which carp darted. At Christmas a decorated tree illuminated the garden.

One of the museum's most important support groups, the Council, was born in 1955 to involve more women in the museum's programs. Dedicated members from many parts of Virginia gave long hours of work, helping to operate the museum gift shop, serving as gallery docents and theatre hostesses, selling Virginia artists' works, raising funds, organizing the Viennese Balls, and expanding the museum library's collection.

Many Council members involved their husbands—busy doctors, lawyers, accountants and bankers—in the museum. Council tours of the galleries were designed to interest husbands in the museum's many activities. "Without the Council I couldn't have got anything done," Cheek later said. "The ladies were invaluable."

Throughout his tenure Cheek produced a rapid-fire series of exhibits covering the arts of all periods. In October of 1955, *Architecture of Japan* brought a viewing of enlarged photo-

ABOVE: Visitors passed through this carpenter Gothic styled pergola to enter *The Tastemakers*, the 1957 exhibition examining changes in American culture since 1840. The use of visually eye-catching motifs like this at the entrance of loan exhibitions was a favorite Cheek strategem. The aim was to select some thematic element from the show which would place the gallery visitor "in the proper mood," as Leslie liked to phrase it. **RIGHT:** *Les Fêtes Galantes* celebrated the museum's acquisition in 1955 of Watteau's *Le Lorgneur*. This photograph shows how Lusklites were used to direct one's attention to the paintings.

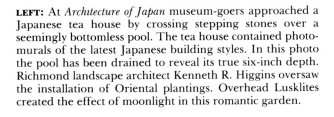

LEFT: At *Architecture of Japan* museum-goers approached a Japanese tea house by crossing stepping stones over a seemingly bottomless pool. The tea house contained photomurals of the latest Japanese building styles. In this photo the pool has been drained to reveal its true six-inch depth. Richmond landscape architect Kenneth R. Higgins oversaw the installation of Oriental plantings. Overhead Lusklites created the effect of moonlight in this romantic garden.

graphs of Japanese buildings. Visitors walked through a Japanese garden to a teahouse, lit by a lantern. An adjoining pool looked deep under artificial moonlight, shed by a combination of amber and blue Lusklites; actually, the illusory pool had only a few inches of water over its black tar paper base. Plants native to the Orient gave authenticity to the water garden. A Richmond press reviewer called the show "an undisputed success."

Cheek called Watteau's painting, *Le Lorgneur*, purchased in 1955, "the most important work of art" the institution had acquired to that time. The museum welcomed it at *Les Fêtes Galantes* in January 1956. Paintings by Watteau's contemporaries—Boucher, Pater, Lancret and Fragonard—were included. They depicted courtiers, courtesans, actors and musicians engaged in the pleasures of 17th and 18th century France.

As an introduction to *Les Fêtes Galantes*, Cheek re-created a Piranesi-inspired ruin—a fallen column, crumbling classical walls, and a fountain fed by water from a toppled urn. Mobiles in the shape of butterflies fluttered overhead. A realistic lizard stuck its head out of a crack in the ruin. Courtly music by Rameau and Scarlatti played softly. A text in faded 18th century script introduced the viewer to the scene, where several objects were placed as if left there by strolling lovers: a blue damask stole, a basket of roses, a book, a fan. The objects came straight from a romantic painting of the Watteau school.

Not all Cheek exhibits depicted the distant past or foreign cultures. *The Tastemakers*, based on Russell Lynes' book of that name, in 1957 contrasted American styles over two centuries. It examined American taste from 1840 to 1957, re-creating typical rooms from several periods. Lynes lectured at the museum during the exhibition. He pronounced it "an extremely handsome show, very imaginatively done . . ."

ABOVE AND LEFT: New York designer Richard Erdoes prepared this gaily colored map, entrance sign and layout for *England's World of 1607*, commemorating the 350th anniversary of the first permanent English settlement at Jamestown. The loan gallery was divided by partitions into smaller display areas topped by symbols of English heraldry. These areas were devoted to the impact of world travel and trade on 17th century English culture.

RIGHT: Costumes (top), once used in a Broadway show, were part of *Theatre Designs by Donald Oenslager*. The 1958 exhibition paid homage to the Yale faculty member who profoundly influenced the career of Leslie Cheek. Entry to the Oenslager exhibition (below), in one of the museum's loan galleries, was had by passing through a rubbish-filled alley to this backstage door, complete with watchman, trash can and realistic stuffed rat (between the bottom step and the trash can). "The biggest thrill of my life is to see what the Virginia Museum has done with my stuff," declared the renowned New York stage designer.

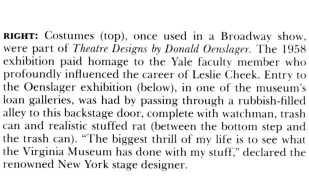

On the 350th anniversary of Virginia's Jamestown settlement in 1957, the museum re-created *England's World of 1607*. It depicted the expansion of British influence and settlement in an age of exploration. Designer Richard Erdoes of New York keynoted the presentation with a bold, graphic map showing trade routes and lands known to Captain John Smith's day. White standards at the museum's entrance bore the Cross of Saint George, which Virginia's first settlers flew at Jamestown. The Museum Theatre simultaneously produced Shakespeare's *The Tempest*, written soon after Jamestown was founded.

When the museum produced *Theatre Designs by Donald Oenslager* in 1958, a lighted sign at the Boulevard entrance flashed on and off like a Broadway marquee. Cheek re-created a stage door entrance to the exhibition, tended by a burly watchman with cigar, green eyeshade, and a copy of *Variety*. Inside were mannequins in Oenslager's Broadway costumes, eighty drawings of his best stage designs, a few models of his work, and a full-size re-creation of his original set for Somerset Maugham's *The Constant Wife*.

A 1958 exhibition of *The Architecture of Skidmore, Owings and Merrill* opened coincident with the dedication of Richmond's newly-completed Reynolds Metals headquarters, designed by the world-famous firm. For the show's preview, 3,000 guests were bused from the museum to the $11.5 million Reynolds building for a tour and cocktail party. A panel of prominent designers, polled for the museum by Frederick Nichols of the University of Virginia, pronounced the Reynolds structure the most significant erected in the Commonwealth since Thomas Jefferson designed the University of Virginia, which dated to 1819.

In these years, Leslie Cheek was often invited to serve on national boards, committees and commissions. He accepted several appointments, including the fine arts committee of the U.S. Air Force Academy in Colorado Springs; the Fine Arts Advisory Committee of President Eisenhower's People-

Leslie Cheek in his office at the museum, 1960.

to-People program, of which he became chairman; and the U.S. exhibition committee to the Brussels World's Fair of 1958.

On February 14, 1958, while Cheek was in Brussels to supervise the American presentation, Virginia newspapers surprised readers with the news that he had resigned as director of the Virginia Museum. It was Cheek's protest against what he thought was unwarranted interference with his administration by the museum's president.

Cheek's action caught his trustees by surprise, for they had come to know him as a highly effective director. Though his methods were often unorthodox, they were undeniably successful. The museum's state appropriation had jumped from $60,000 in 1948 to nearly $250,000 in 1958. Membership had risen from 1,000 in 1948 to ten times that number in a decade. Endowment for art purchases stood at $5,000,000.

When Cheek returned to Richmond from Brussels, he met with the trustees over a two week period in an effort to resolve his differences with the president. At last an agreement was reached. Leslie Cheek would return to his post, and the museum president would decline re-election. In May, a new president was chosen, John Garland Pollard, Jr., whose father had been largely responsible for creating the Virginia Museum as governor from 1930 to 1934. He and Cheek would work well together.

The shocking news of Cheek's resignation had provoked a flood of letters and telephone calls to the museum. Nearly all urged the director to stay on the job. The welcome announcement that he would do so was widely hailed by newspaper editorials and television commentators. It seemed that Cheek had become a legend in his own time: a symbol of Virginia's dedication to the arts as essential to the good life.

As Leslie Cheek entered the last half of his twenty-year Virginia directorship, his most spectacular triumphs still lay ahead. He was indeed the right man in the right place at the right time. □

The Virginia Museum Theatre's production of Rodgers and Hammerstein's *The King and I* (1963) was one of many popular musicals staged at the museum. These elegant sets were designed by John Döepp.

CHAPTER IX

The Virginia Museum Theatre
BRANCHING OUT

Leslie Cheek's interest in the stage began in his childhood in Nashville. As a boy, he had staged puppet shows for his sister, and he frequently dressed up in the native costumes of Germans and Scots which his Grandmother Wood brought from trips abroad. There were also outings to local vaudeville shows with his father and attendance with his mother at Metropolitan Opera productions when they came to Nashville each spring.

In college and as a teacher at William and Mary, Leslie continued to indulge his zeal for the theatre. At the Baltimore Museum he had introduced drama, music and dance to enliven its program. Thus it seemed only natural that when the Virginia Museum's new director learned that the state had approved proposals for the gallery's expansion, he began lobbying to include a theatre.

But first he had to persuade the museum's board of trustees why a theatre was necessary. Cheek saw all the arts as the museum's potential realm. As he told a *Richmond News Leader* reporter upon his arrival in Richmond in 1948, "Museums should be conducted so that they will become as necessary as a fire department or a public library." He felt they should be a place for the enjoyment of all creativity.

Fortunately, Cheek was able to convince the board that a theatre would add to the museum as a cultural center.

When the state voted funds for constructing the North Wing, it stipulated that none could be used to build a theatre. Furthermore, once it began operating, the theatre would have to pay the Commonwealth rental fees for the use of museum facilities. Cheek overcame these problems by raising private funds to build the structure.

Cheek chose top designers to create an ideal multi-use theatre. Edward Cole designed the stage and stage house, Stanley McCandless the lighting, and George Izenour the lighting and sound control systems. Designer Florence "Shu" Knoll of New York styled the interior.

OPPOSITE PAGE: The 550-seat auditorium opened in October of 1955, through the support of the Old Dominion Foundation. The technically advanced theatre could be curtained off to create a more intimate space for lectures, workshops and concerts. **ABOVE:** The crowded theatre lobby at intermission. Cheek later opened museum galleries so theatre-goers could see the latest exhibitions during these 30-minute pauses.

ABOVE RIGHT: The Izenour Control Panel for the theatre's state-of-the-art lighting and sound systems. **RIGHT:** Dedicated volunteers worked tirelessly behind the scenes building sets for *The Miracle Worker* (1967).

Maxwell Anderson's *High Tor*, the first play (1955).

The Imaginary Invalid (1958), by Molière.

The cost of the theatre, nearly $1 million, was borne by Paul Mellon's Old Dominion Foundation. The foundation's initial gift of $250,000 was given in 1950, but more was needed. "We had built the auditorium," Cheek recalled later, "but could not afford to build the stage house with its curtains, scenery, and lighting switchboard system."

Fortunately for Virginia, Mr. and Mrs. Mellon paid a visit in 1954 to the unfinished theatre wing. "Why aren't you going on with the stage?" Mrs. Mellon asked Cheek. "Because we don't have enough money," the director replied. "Well," Mrs. Mellon said, "that seems a pity."

The next day Mellon's lawyer phoned from Washington and asked Cheek how much would it cost to finish the job. Cheek told him $650,000. Two weeks later the lawyer phoned again and said, "Go ahead and finish it."

The Rockefeller Foundation also made a grant to help meet the theatre's operating costs in its early years. The building was soon underway.

The 550-seat auditorium turned out to be a jewel. Cheek's team designed the stage with a high loft so that sets could be quickly lifted up and shifted beyond the view of the audience. To do this without heightening the museum's roofline, the stage had to be placed well below ground level. The theatre's stage and other equipment were more sophisticated than those of most Broadway theaters. It was one of the most advanced theatres of its kind in the nation. The auditorium walls were covered in Prussian blue book-binders' cloth, with a salmon colored velvet curtain across its wide stage. The theatre was equipped for plays, musicals, dance recitals and lectures. An orchestra pit for 36 musicians could rise or descend at the press of a button. Divider curtains could partition the auditorium into a more intimate 300-seats if desired. The lighting and sound control booth was placed above and to the rear of the auditorium to give technicians a sweeping view of performances.

The galleries in the new theatre wing were opened in the fall of 1954, but the theatre was not opened until October 1955, with a musical performance by the Amadeus Quartet.

To direct the theatre, Cheek engaged veteran Vincent Bowditch, a Harvard graduate who had worked with the Pasadena Playhouse and other stock companies. Bowditch's difficult task was to create a community theatre with performers and production crew from unpaid volunteers. The only paid theater workers in the beginning, besides Bowditch, were set designer Ariel Ballif, and technical director Joseph Carner.

The Museum Theatre was a success, thanks in part to the many enthusiastic volunteers—some of professional training and ability—who acted and worked backstage. They formed the Virginia Museum Theatre Associates and leavened their work by staging cast parties and an annual Parody Ball. Guests came in costumes spoofing their favorite role. One couple in 1959 dressed up as two tables, taking off the season's production of *Separate Tables*.

The Museum Theatre launched its first season in 1955 with Maxwell Anderson's *High Tor*. Ballif's set, portraying the rugged peak of a mountain half-obscured by clouds and fog (generated backstage by smoke bombs and dry ice) set the theatre's high technical standards. Sometimes, Cheek realized, the scenery and stage effects overshadowed the performers onstage.

Before he left the Museum Theatre in 1959, Ballif created memorable designs for such plays as *Lute Song*, the nine mobile hangings for which changed with each scene, and for *Victoria Regina*, which used a specially-built revolving stage to permit fifteen rapid scene shifts. For a production of Karel Capek's science-fiction melodrama, *R.U.R.*, Ballif got his inspiration from "Flash Gordon" and other futuristic comic strips. Shakespeare's *The Tempest* in 1957 was the first VMT production inspired by an exhibition at the museum—in this case, *England's World of 1607*.

In 1961 when the museum celebrated its 25th anniversary with the exhibition *Treasures*

Cole Porter's *Kiss Me, Kate*, the first musical (1959).

The Six Degrees of Crime (1961), by Frederic Hill.

Samuel Beckett's *Waiting for Godot* (1962).

Richard Sheridan's *The School for Scandal* (1963).

in America, the Museum Theatre offered an inspired production of Sheridan's 18th century comedy, *She Stoops to Conquer.* In 1963, *The School for Scandal* similarly accompanied the exhibition *Painting in England.*

The theatre opened at a time of nationwide racial tensions, which were strongly felt in Richmond. The Supreme Court in 1954 had handed down its historic decision ending racial segregation in the public schools. Despite the edict, some VMT patrons felt that the Museum Theatre should segregate the races in its audiences. Leslie Cheek thought otherwise. Wrote Vincent Bowditch later, "Leslie proposed, and I fully concurred . . . that the audience be seated without regard to the segregation issue . . . Leslie was far ahead of his time in accepting . . . the reality . . . of justice for all."

When Bowditch resigned as theatre director after two years, exhausted, he was replaced briefly by Arthur Ballet. Like Bowditch, he tried to operate the theatre without financial loss, despite the fact that the Rockefeller Foundation grant continued to cover the small annual shortfall. However, when the 1958 season resulted in a deficit of $27,000, Ballet resigned.

Cheek still believed his concept for the theatre was sound. He felt that what had been lacking was leadership to make it work. In Robert Telford, Cheek found a particularly imaginative and gifted director. A graduate of the Yale Drama School, Telford had been head of the Town Theatre in Columbia, South Carolina. He felt the VMT should move away from its usual run of serious plays, and should include a few Broadway musicals. In the museum's 1959-60 *Annual Report,* Cheek wrote: "The choice of plays was geared to enlarging the public awareness of the VMT through popular, but appropriate productions."

The first musical, *Kiss Me, Kate,* opened the 1959-60 season. It was a resounding success. All performances were sold out, and extra ones were scheduled to meet the public demand. Telford later wrote that:

The opening night must have been traumatic for Cheek. Part of the scenery got caught and was raised and lowered several times and at a perilous angle, the light system blew a fuse and we played several scenes with just a follow spot which was on a different circuit while tech people raced through the underground areas to repair the situation . . . Somehow the audience enjoyed itself tremendously. While I suffered—and Cheek undoubtedly died—they applauded the songs, the dancing, the play and even the bungled scene and light changes. Late that evening when the opening night festivities were over—I was hiding in a corner in the Members' Suite receiving plaudits from the audience and hoping Cheek was receiving the same—he sidled up to my wife and me and said, rather obliquely, 'Well, I hear you have a hit.' I must say that those were the most gratifying words of the evening.

During Telford's directorship the popular musicals continued: *Carousel, Paint Your Wagon,* and *Fanny,* just to name a few. Other productions were *Hamlet, Hedda Gabler, Waiting for Godot,* and *The Visit.* Critics invariably praised the excellent sets and costumes, which were the work of William Ryan, another Yale School of Drama graduate who came to the theatre the same year as Telford. In 1963 Cheek made Ryan the museum's exhibition designer after the sudden death of the talented John Koenig. Ryan's theatre post was filled by John Döepp. Hansford Rowe served as Telford's able assistant during these years.

For seven years Robert Telford lifted the theatre to its greatest popularity and box office success. Operating deficits were reduced, and in 1963, 1964, and 1965 the theatre posted small surpluses.

For each production, Cheek insisted on a 30-minute intermission between acts, so that theatre goers could stroll through the galleries and see the exhibitions.

Hansford Rowe, who went from the Museum Theatre to Broadway, says that "Mr. Cheek was ubiquitous. He oversaw the grand scheme of things and the tiniest of details. He delegated authority, but kept an eye out for the final product." And Robert Telford adds, "I'm told that the success or failure of my

Dark of the Moon (1967), by Richardson and Berney.

Molière's *The School for Wives* (1967).

141

Carousel (1960), by Rodgers and Hammerstein.

Hamlet (1964), by William Shakespeare.

plays was measured during the twelve seconds after the curtain first went up. During those twelve seconds, [Cheek] scrutinized the set—every cornice!—and either relaxed or began making copious notes. These were put to paper—1-½ by 2-½ inch—later that night and arrived on my desk the next morning."

Designer Jack Döepp recalls:

We were planning a production of Moliere's *Tartuffe* and bringing in the British actor Eric Christmas to direct and star. A big event. I had finished the preliminary drawings for the show and Eric had approved them. I was pleased and we all proceeded . . . to show them to Mr. Cheek who said after due deliberation, 'This looks like a Park Avenue apartment.' So back I went, feathers ruffled, to the drawing board. After diligent research and a more sensitive look into the 18th century, I resubmitted the drawings which were blessedly approved. Looking back at the original design it indeed *did* look like a Park Avenue apartment. The product onstage was unquestionably an improvement over the original.

The Museum Theatre was the site for many activities. An annual film series was screened there, and lecturers spoke from the stage. The museum's guest speakers reads like a Who's Who of the art world: Arthur Drexler, John Walker, Philip Adams, Henry-Russell Hitchcock, Buckminster Fuller, Sir Herbert Read, Richard Neutra, Harris Prior, Thomas Messer, W.G. Constable, Will Barnet, Lloyd Goodrich and others.

Music and dance occupied the theatre too on seasonal programs offered by the museum. The Museum Theatre was also the site for the Virginia College Drama Festival each February, playing host to troupes from Virginia colleges and universities for a day of workshops, professional lectures, and one-act plays critiqued by Broadway experts. Among the guest speakers were playwright Marc Connelly, stage designer Jo Meilziner, critics Norris Houghton and Stella Adler, and producer Alfred de Liagre. The museum also sponsored a less successful College Dance Festival.

Paint Your Wagon (1961), by Lerner and Loewe.

Life with Mother (1962), by Lindsay and Crouse.

Molière's *Tartuffe* (1964).

J. M. Barrie's *The Admirable Chrichton* (1965).

To mark the theatre's tenth anniversary in 1965, the museum collected audio taped congratulations of an impressive roster of stars. Museum publicist William Morrison arranged this tribute, recording greetings by such celebrities as Henry Fonda (Cheek's roommate at Cape Cod in the summer of 1930), Olivia deHavilland, Lee Remick (whose father had been a Harvard classmate of Cheek's), John Forsythe and Angela Lansbury. Videotaped announcements were made by Gregory Peck, Shirley MacLaine and Helen Hayes. The greetings were made available to radio and television stations and widely broadcast.

Robert Telford resigned as theatre director in June 1966 to direct the Scott Repertory Company in Fort Worth, Texas. He was succeeded by James Dyas. In July, president Walter Robertson announced that the museum had been awarded federal matching funds to create a professional drama center. Cheek persuaded then Governor Mills E. Godwin, Jr., to designate the Virginia Museum as the state's *pro tem* arts council, since it encompassed the largest professional arts program in the Commonwealth. With this designation, the museum qualified for $50,000 in federal funds for the arts, and enlarged its statewide drama activities.

Called the Virginia Museum Theatre Arts System, the program was initiated in the fall of 1966, with Frank Gilroy's Pulitzer prize winning play, *The Subject was Roses*. It performed in twenty Virginia localities, with a professional cast and paid stagehands. From this time onward, the Museum Theatre began to depend more on paid professionals.

In the season of 1967-68, the Museum Theatre for the first time could afford to offer Virginia a program of theatre, dance and music on tour and at the building itself.

Of all Cheek's Virginia Museum innovations, the introduction of the performing arts proved the most difficult. Yet it achieved his goal of attracting a wider range of people to the arts. Other museums were to follow Virginia's lead in introducing the performing arts. Cheek's years at the museum were a golden age for the theatre in Virginia. □

In 1962 Artmobile II took *Twelve Portraits: Delacroix to Gauguin* across the state. These French paintings were in the colleciton of Paul Mellon of Upperville, whose generosity made possible the Virginia Museum's second Artmobile. In 1985 Mr. Mellon gave the museum Auguste Renoir's *The Artist's Son Jean* (middle row, far right) and Edgar Degas' *Madame Julie Burtin* (top row, far left). Today, museum policy prohibits displaying unprotected paintings in the open air, as was done for this publicity photo. (Courtesy: *Life Magazine,* © 1962 Time Inc.)

CHAPTER X

The Virginia Museum
BEARING FRUIT 1960-1965

Arts in Virginia · Nineteen hundred and sixty AIV '60

The magazine *Arts in Virginia* (or *AIV*) was begun in 1961, part of the museum's 25th anniversary promotional campaign, and is still published to this day. Its first issue (left) carried an article by future Virginia Museum director Paul N. Perrot. The thrice-yearly publication has consistently won awards for its distinctive design and layout. **ABOVE:** Cheek confers with staff members William Rhodes, William Francis (*AIV* editor from 1961-68), Joseph Watson (*AIV* designer from 1964-68) and Paul Grigaut. Leslie surrounded himself with talented men and women who gave the museum their all.

AIV 63

The 1960s were turbulent years in America, stained by the assassination of President John Kennedy and by other violence. For the Virginia Museum, however, they were years of unprecedented triumphs. To Leslie Cheek, who turned 52 in 1960, they brought the fulfillment of plans he had worked at ever since he took over the directorship of the nation's first state-supported art museum in 1948.

The decade was keynoted by the museum's 25th anniversary in 1961. Since its creation in 1936 at the intersection of Richmond's Boulevard and Grove Avenue, the institution had expanded Americans' concept of what the arts could do to make life more rewarding. Now the imaginative Cheek unveiled new avenues of growth.

To plan the anniversary, Cheek and the museum's trustees obtained the counsel of New York publicist Earl Newsome and his media specialists. They sought to widen the museum's usefulness through the press, radio, television and films. To proclaim the birthday, six Virginia newspapers carried a 12-page museum anniversary supplement. The museum printed a new brochure of its services, and it commissioned producer Richard de Rochement, formerly of *The March of Time,* to create a 25-minute color documentary motion picture titled *Museum in Action* for theatres, television and use by groups.

The film was widely acclaimed especially for its narration by British journalist Alistair Cooke. He jauntily described his first unexpected view of the Artmobile on a Virginia highway and his resultant discovery of the museum responsible for it. He talked glowingly of the institution's changing exhibits, its lively theatre, its art classes for all ages, and its wealth of lectures and performances.

By this time Cheek had succeeded in opening the museum at night, and attendance grew. Audiences at night events in the museum theatre—lectures, concerts, films and five or six plays presented from eight to thirty times apiece—especially welcomed the innovation. The United States Information Agency in Washington asked Cheek to describe his unusual museum in a round-the-world broadcast.

Concerned always about its obligation to outlying Virginians, the museum launched in 1961 a thrice-yearly magazine called *Arts in Virginia,* or *AIV.* The graphically innovative journal explored the arts of past and present in pictures and articles by staff members and outside specialists.

In a further effort to extend its outreach, the museum in 1960 began to create museum chapters of interested citizens outside Richmond. By September 1961 it had 17 chapters and affiliates. To them the museum provided Artmobile visits, art shows, and painting and drawing classes. Leslie and Mary Tyler visited some chapters and were usually at the museum in Richmond to receive chapter "safaris." These included gallery tours, theatre performances, and lunches and dinners in the Medieval Hall. Through its chapters the museum widened its membership from 3,600 people in 1960 to 6,400 in 1962.

Along with its rising state appropriations support, Cheek saw that the museum needed more private giving. Gallery visitors paid only a small admission, while the subsidized theatre operated at an annual loss, except for the years 1963-65. To widen its gifts, the director in 1960 proposed a new organization. He wrote president John Garland Pollard, Jr., of "our need for . . . a separate, new endowment . . . perhaps entitled 'The Fellows of the Virginia Museum,' with yearly contributions and special gifts . . ."

Cheek had been developing the plan since 1955, when the trustees first tentatively endorsed it. Accordingly, The Fellows of the Virginia Museum was created in 1961, when president Walter S. Robertson, Pollard's successor, invited public-spirited Paul Mellon to be first chairman. "We conceive The Fellows as a most important group," Cheek wrote Mellon.

[O]ur 25th Anniversary Program has been so successful that we are nearly swamped with requests for increased art services all over the State. To meet this hoped-for challenge, we shall need advice and aid from private sources, since public sources cannot operate quickly enough to grasp the many opportunities . . . As our Museum now enters a phase of great expansion of its State Services, it needs the

TREASURES
IN
AMERICA

A SPECIAL EXHIBITION OF
MASTERPIECES TO HONOR
THE 25TH BIRTHDAY OF THE
VIRGINIA MUSEUM AND TO
PAY TRIBUTE TO THE ART
COLLECTORS OF AMERICA

COLLECTORS OF AMERICA

immediate backing and counsel . . . of leaders with fine education, broad experience and mellowed taste to guide the Museum into its larger opportunities ahead . . .

Cheek emphasized that "It is a *national* group we are seeking," and that "operation of the society will be as informal as possible." Each Fellow would contribute at least $250 yearly and be available to give advice to the museum. The concept assured long-range support for the institution and its many activities.

The Fellows convened for the first time in April 1961. Each spring thereafter, they met, dined and were entertained at the museum before journeying the next day to a plantation or historic house for luncheon. Raymond Guest of Powhatan plantation in northern Virginia, succeeded Paul Mellon as The Fellows' second chairman, followed by Admiral Lewis Strauss of Culpeper. In Cheek's years, The Fellows gave more than $200,000 to a number of important projects, including creating the museum's gallery orientation theatres, making possible statewide tours of theatrical productions, and planning the museum's growth.

As the *piece de résistance* for the museum's birthday in 1961, Cheek produced a monumental exhibition, *Treasures in America*. It was made up of the best works from Oriental, European and classical antiquity to the present, borrowed from top American museums.

The collection included works by El Greco, Ingres, Cezanne and Winslow Homer. A memorable catalogue contained essays by Harris Prior, president of the American Federation of Arts, and by Alfred Frankfurter of *Art News*.

A twenty-fifth birthday ball on February 17, 1961, brought 500 of the museum's best friends and top officialdom, including Governor J. Lindsay Almond, Jr. After a candlelit dinner in the Medieval Hall, the museum presented awards to five major arts contributors: architect Eero Saarinen, the late sculptor

Treasures in America opened in January, 1961, and commemorated the museum's first twenty-five years. This important exhibition was a tribute to America's leading collectors and patrons of art. Included were objects from ancient to modern times.

In 1961 the museum unveiled its permanent Egyptian Gallery, a gift of Mrs. James Parsons of Richmond. **TOP:** Cheek recreated a dimly lit tomb with a ramp, along which were lined statuary. **BOTTOM:** Awed visitors gazed down on this ransacked tomb, complete with unwrapped mummy (right) from the IX-XI Dynasties. In 1984 the museum placed the mummy back in its sarcophagus and closed the lid, much to the disappointment of children.

Carl Milles, collector Robert Lehman of New York, naval designer William Gibbs, and the Old Dominion Foundation. Two beautiful models, dressed in Degas ballet dresses, wheeled a 4-foot-tall birthday cake into the room for Governor Almond to cut.

Cheek had long sought an Egyptian Gallery, and in April 1961 he got one. It was created on one side of the Mediterranean Court built in 1953-54. Given by Mrs. James Parsons of Richmond, the installation was designed by Cheek to depict the tomb of an Egyptian pharoah. The gallery simulated a sloping masonry passage, dimly lit, lined with Egyptian statuary. It led upward to a low-ceilinged corridor where other pharaonic objects were on view.

At the end of the corridor an open shaft revealed a small burial chamber, ten feet below. There, in Cheek's re-creation, lay an Egyptian mummy, recently acquired from New York's Metropolitan Museum. The chamber appeared to have been ransacked by robbers, as many Egyptian tombs were. The lid of the mummy case was ajar, exposing the unwrapped body within. Canopic jars and tomb furnishings were strewn nearby.

To prepare the Egyptian gallery, Cheek spent hours over his drawing board. ("He was always happiest over that board," recalled Mary Tyler.) He took the design from an Egyptian tomb excavated in 1923 by the Boston Museum. To the exhibit's walls and floor he applied gritty paint to simulate granite. Calling on his scenic design and camouflage experience, he made plywood walls look like huge stones. To create an eerie mood, he had Egyptian music played softly over the gallery's sound system.

To open the Egyptian Gallery in April 1961, Cheek dressed waiters in the flowing white gowns of Egyptian dragomen, with bare feet and red fezzes, and gave them trays of drinks to serve. If guests asked what the drinks were, Cheek instructed them to say it was embalming fluid. It didn't faze the thirsty guests.

The exhibit was a hit with adults and

children, who were awed to silence as they formed a single file line and went in to view the mummy, which the staff had named "Theby." Docents from the Museum Council were often amused by childrens' comments at their first sight of the mummy. "A daid man!" one boy exclaimed. "Who kilt him?"

How had the Virginia Museum managed to acquire such rare and sought-after Egyptian objects? Several museums asked that question. The answer was that Cheek had utilized the expertise of one of the world's top Egyptologists to acquire it. He was Bernard Bothmer, whom Cheek had known at the Boston Museum before Bothmer became a curator at Egypt's archaelogical museum in Cairo. Bothmer helped the museum acquire the best Egyptian collection to be found in any American gallery south of Baltimore.

In the same way, Cheek engaged Metropolitan Museum and Walters Gallery curators who had retired, to help the museum to obtain unique Oriental, Ancient Greek, Byzantine and Near East collections. Their findings were displayed in a triumphant succession of Virginia Museum exhibitions during the 1960s, before being added to the institution's permanent collections.

When the centennial of the Civil War approached in 1961, the city of Richmond planned a civic observance to call attention to its key role as the Confederacy's capital from 1861-1865. Cheek was a member of the Richmond committee helping to plan a large and festive Centennial Center for Richmond, designed by modernist architect Walter Dorwin Teague. When criticized by one city councilman as "a grapefruit turned upside down over a doughnut," Cheek replied that it was "useful, functional and quite handsome." The Teague entry was ultimately built, and eventually became a facility of Virginia Commonwealth University.

The Virginia Museum's own contribution to the Civil War centennial was an exhibit of 19th century arts and social history titled *Home Front, 1861.* The main gallery re-created a moon-lit 1861 Richmond garden with an

The Virginia Museum joined in the festivities marking the Civil War Centennial. *Home Front, 1861* provided relief for those weary of hearing about nothing but battlefields and generals. This exhibition examined domestic life on the eve of the War Between the States through painting, decorative arts, fashion and theatre. The courtyard (above) invoked the charming antebellum gardens of Richmond. Cheek borrowed the fountain from St. Paul's Church, where it is in use today. In the rebuilt dwelling were examples of 19th century fashion and furnishings. In the loan gallery (right) was a collection of Currier and Ives prints recording everyday life in pre-Civil War America. The pot-bellied stove contained lifelike embers which realistically glowed.

ABOVE: *Painting in England 1700-1850* was the largest single exhibition ever held at the Virginia Museum. Every gallery was cleared to make room for Paul Mellon's enormous collection of British art. Over 400 masterpieces by such artists as Turner, Constable, Hogarth and Blake dazzled museum-goers between April and August of 1963. **BELOW:** Leslie Cheek and Paul Mellon examine Francis Wheatley's *Family Group* before the opening. Basil Taylor, Mr. Mellon's adviser and Librarian of London's Royal College of Art, prepared the two-volume catalogue, one of the cover's for which (right) featured a detail from Stubbs' *Phaeton with Cream Ponies and Stable-Lad*.

PAINTING IN ENGLAND 1700-1850

COLLECTION OF MR & MRS PAUL MELLON
VIRGINIA MUSEUM OF FINE ARTS 1963

operating cast-iron fountain, plus urns and benches. Adjoining it was an exhibit of photographs of ante-bellum houses, gardens and public buildings, some of them still standing in downtown Richmond. Typical Richmond rooms were decorated in styles popular in the Civil War: neo-Gothic, Victorian, and Louis XV and XVI. Within the rooms, mannequins displayed Civil War costumes from the Valentine Museum's collection.

A grand gallery of 19th century style exhibited the arts of the period. The best paintings were by George Innes, Albert Bierstadt and Winslow Homer, while popular art was shown in a reconstructed Currier and Ives print gallery. Here a pot-bellied stove lent authenticity, with a long black metal pipe for ventilation, and fake embers flickered realistically through the stove's isinglass window.

As a feature of *Home Front, 1861*, the Virginia Museum Theatre produced *The Six Degrees of Crime*, a melodrama from the gaslit age that Cheek had earlier unearthed for his *Romanticism in America* exhibition held in 1940 at the Baltimore Museum. During intermission playgoers could stroll through the *Home Front* exhibit. There they found costumed vendors hawking patent medicine and gold bricks—remnants of a credulous age. That Leslie Cheek thought of everything!

One bittersweet comment from an anonymous visitor at this period survived in the museum's guest book: "In this miserable state of Virginia where all culture is stunted due [to] its petty preoccupation with those by-gone days of the Civil War, this place is a breath of relief from the 'Y'all come see the General Lee monuments.' "

In 1962 the Council opened the museum's first gift shop. Founded by Mrs. Warwick Davenport, Mrs. John Pearsall and Mrs. Eugene Sydnor, it offered books, postcards, crafts and art reproductions. These were sold from movable carts which Leslie designed and became the Council's greatest source of income. Profits were given by the Council to expand the museum library. The carts served until a larger shop was included in the muse-

The Greek Line, 1962. Attic kylikes purchased by the museum with the help of adviser Christine Alexander were mounted on pedestals before photo enlargements of the scenes painted on the vases. One of these terra cotta vases was accidentally broken during the exhibition, but was repaired by conservators.

um's new North Wing, completed in 1976. The Council and the gift shop became essential features of the museum.

Cheek made a second attempt in 1962 to work with Hollywood in developing an exhibition on film-making. Through his friend Frank McCarthy, a Richmonder who became a movie producer, he decided to build the exhibit around director George Stevens and his spectacular biblical film, *The Greatest Story Ever Told.* Cheek even sent designer William Ryan to Hollywood in 1965 to work with Stevens. Unfortunately, the project had to be cancelled a few weeks before opening when the museum was unable to raise its $34,000 operating cost. Twenty years later, the Smithsonian Institution originated a similar show, which was to tour the United States, France and Japan.

In 1963 the museum gave America its first view of Paul Mellon's newly-acquired collection. The show was *Painting in England, 1700-1850.* Mellon said he had been inspired to collect it by the museum's 1960 *Sport and the Horse,* of which he had been chairman. The 400 paintings, watercolors and sketches, including many by John Constable, Thomas Gainsborough, J.M.W. Turner and George Stubbs, overran every gallery in the museum. For the first time visitors could use LecTour, an earphone guide system. A two-volume catalogue by Basil Taylor, Mellon's adviser for his English acquisitions, accompanied the show. Sheridan's *The School for Scandal* was the Museum Theatre's production. The Mellon exhibition ran for a record five months.

The exhibition strengthened ties between the museum and Mellon, its greatest benefactor. "Many, many thanks to Leslie," Paul Mellon wrote Mary Tyler Cheek, "who did so much to put on such a fine and attractive show, and who had so much to do with the

setting (and so many headaches and time limits and movings and personal problems) . . ."

The museum joined in an international observance in 1963 of the 40th anniversary of the discovery by Howard Carter of King Tut's tomb. The museum's loan exhibition, *Treasures of Tutankhamun,* drew so many spectators that a line-up extended through the museum doors to the parking lot outside. The art was shown in a replica of a darkened tomb wherein Egyptian objects rested on pedestals, each illuminated by a narrow beam of light.

Greek Gold, held in 1966, similarly featured dramatic lighting techniques. Hellenic treasures, assembled jointly with the Boston and Brooklyn museums, were shown in cases lit by tiny spotlights, inspired by the displays at Tiffany's of New York.

Always popular with Anglophile Virginians were Cheek's exhibits of British art and social history. Three favorites of the 1960s were *William Hogarth, Festival Designs by Inigo Jones,* and *William Blake: Poet, Painter, Prophet.*

To display its fifteen newly-acquired Greek terra cotta vases from the fifth and sixth centuries, Cheek in 1962 unveiled an exhibition titled *The Greek Line.* The vases, hand-painted in black and burnt orange to depict Greek battles and athletic contests, had been opportunely obtained by the museum through the efforts of Christine Alexander, a retired Metropolitan Museum curator. Like Bernard Bothmer, she was an expert Cheek engaged part-time. Using her specialized knowledge, Virginia's young museum had secured rare and valuable works in Cheek's years before larger institutions noticed them.

In addition to Christine Alexander and Bernard Bothmer, the museum was also helped by Marvin Ross, who had retired as curator of Byzantine art at the Walters Gallery in Baltimore, and Allen Priest, formerly of the Metropolitan, who advised on Oriental art.

While on exhibit in *The Greek Line,* one priceless Hellenic kylix was knocked from its supporting pedestal and shattered. The mishap upset the museum staff and received newspaper headlines. It happened when a

visitor backed into the pedestal bearing the vase, which had stood out against a photographic enlargement of its design, stunningly shown in a gallery painted the burnt orange hue of the vases. To Cheek's relief, the damaged kylix was eventually put together flawlessly by an expert conservator.

Cheek's ultilization of specialized advice was welcomed by curator Pinkney Near in expanding the museum's collection. "Leslie Cheek had the ability to surround himself with those who could help . . . like Ross and Priest," Near said later. "He had a sense of his own limits but was smart enough to get high-calibre people to advise him."

Besides the Greek vases, which had been bought from the Lanckoronski collection of Greek antiquities, the museum's endowment in the 1960s made possible other purchases recommended by its curatorial advisers. Through Allen Priest it bought a group of Japanese painted screens from the year 1500 and later. A Tosa Mitsunobu screen in the group is one of the world's finest outside Japan. Similarly, on Marvin Ross' advice, the museum acquired a sought-after 750-year-old stained glass window from England's Canterbury Cathedral.

Ross also helped the museum secure a Byzantine art collection which Near called "one of the three or four best in the country, on par with those at the Walters Gallery and the Dumbarton Oaks collection." He pointed out that:

> All these things were acquired when [the Virginia Museum] had virtually no curatorial staff. The basis of it was the advisers, and the liberality Mr. Cheek gave them. The museum's collections have not known such growth either before or since as during those years, and it is remarkable that we accomplished so much with such little expense in such a brief period.

But the museum's greatest stroke of luck in Cheek's tenure was the discovery in Egypt of part of an alabaster figure previously acquired by the museum. The fragment was found by Bernard Bothmer on a visit to Luxor. It permitted the museum in Richmond

Sculpture by Henry Moore introduced Virginians to the *oeuvre* of one of the world's greatest modern sculptors. A museum staff member traveled to Moore's home in Britain to interview him. The Virginia Museum currently owns two of the artist's abstract works.

After thirteen years of diligent searching, Bernard Bothmer of the Brooklyn Museum united the top half of the Virginia Museum's Egyptian sculpture, *Seated Scribe, Sema-tawy-tefnakht*, with its missing bottom half. The torso, dating to the 7th century B.C., had been purchased in 1951 through The Williams Fund. Bothmer, shown here with the united alabaster figure, found the lower part in 1960 buried in cow dung behind the shop of an antiques dealer in Luxor.

to put back together the two parts of a 7th century BC Egyptian sculpture of a seated scribe long broken and separated.

Bothmer's search for the fragment began after he first visited the Virginia Museum, where he saw the torso fragment in its gallery. On his following visits to Egypt he kept an eye open for the missing lower part. He finally found it half-buried in cow dung behind the shop of an antiquities dealer in Luxor. Even then it took four years of negotiations with the Egyptian government to export the fragment to Virginia. The museum called the resulting exhibition *A Scribe Reseated.* Bothmer's sleuthing received national press attention.

In 1964 the Virginia Museum noted the 400th anniversary of Shakespeare's birth with an exhibition on Elizabethan England, *The World of Shakespeare.* It produced *Hamlet* simultaneously in the Museum Theatre.

For another exhibition, *Homer and the Sea,* Cheek hung fishing nets through the loan galleries and played recordings of sea birds' cries as background for a display of Winslow Homer's seascapes. The pungent odor of caulking tar wafted through the air to invoke the atmosphere of docks and sailing ships.

With a gift from The Fellows, Cheek in the 1960s realized his desire to create small orientation theatres at the entrance to each gallery. These gave the viewer a quick introduction through recorded narration and slides. Frederick Brandt of the museum staff traveled widely and made 7,000 slides of art works, artists and related scenes. The orientation slide talks proved highly popular and became an established exhibition technique.

The museum under Cheek published exhibition catalogues and other books in addition to its magazine, *AIV.* In 1966 the director called a statewide meeting of preservationists to announce the museum's plan to publish *Architecture in Virginia,* an illustrated handbook of major buildings in Virginia since 1607. It was compiled by William B. O'Neal, professor of architectural history at the University of Virginia. The finished work, now out of print, recorded more than 250 build-

Cheek's logo for the Virginia Museum, which he conceived in the mid-1960s, has appeared on matchbooks, stationery, and Council Shop bags, as well as on flatwear and china used in the Members' Suite.

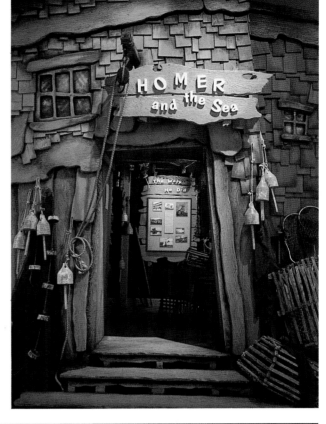

RIGHT: For *Homer and the Sea,* Cheek recreated the sites, sounds and even the smells of the seashore. Winslow Homer seascapes were the subject of this 1964 exhibition. Fishing nets were hung overhead, the cries of gulls were piped in over the audio system, and the odor of tar wafted through the gallery. "Art should be fun," Cheek was fond of saying.
BELOW: Lusklites illumine portraits from Elizabethan England for *The World of Shakespeare,* celebrating the 400th anniversary of the poet-playwright's birth.

THE VIRGINIA MUSEUM OF FINE ARTS
INSIDE: Original paintings displayed
OUTSIDE: Ready to receive visitors
This is a Virginia ARTMOBILE, a complete gallery-on-wheels, and part of the world's first Statewide arts system regularly carrying exhibitions of rare art objects to towns & cities throughout Virginia.
VIRGINIA MUSEUM

A Virginia Museum Artmobile passes the reviewing stand in the Inaugural Parade for President Lyndon B. Johnson, January, 1965. President Johnson and Vice-President Hubert H. Humphrey (standing in the box beneath the Great Seal) applaud as the vehicle rumbles past. David Yerkes, Leslie's friend from Yale and the Army, suggested that the Artmobile be included in the parade, broadcast live on nationwide television.

BELOW: Actor Vincent Price was named "Collector of the Year" in 1965 by the Collectors' Circle, one of many support groups established during Cheek's directorship. Here Price is shown presenting *Sketch of a Woman* by Gaston Lachaise to the museum. Each year the Circle honored a leading American art patron at an elegant dinner served in the Medieval Hall. **RIGHT:** The ladies of the Museum Council organized a "Viennese Ball" for several years during the 1960s to raise money for its various projects. Here the Mediterrean Court has been transformed into a romantic ballroom. At one of these galas a guest who had imbibed too much actually strolled through this fountain pool.

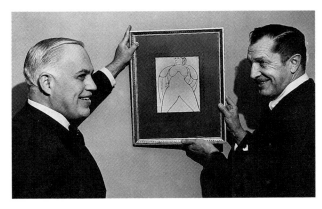

ings in photographs and text.

"Art should be fun," Cheek liked to say, and the energy of his efforts attracted constant attention. He was interviewed by arts commentator Aline Saarinen in 1964 on an NBC television program, *Sunday.* By invitation of the presidential inaugural committee, a Virginia Museum Artmobile paraded through Washington at the inauguration of Lyndon B. Johnson in January 1965. Mrs. Johnson also chose the Virginia Museum as one of twelve institutions to lend works the same year to her White House Festival of the Arts.

Cheek served on a jury of eleven museum heads to choose photographs for the Kodak Pavilion at the 1965 New York World's Fair. The jury members were photographed by famed portrait photographer Yousuf Karsh and appeared both in the Kodak exhibit and later in a book *Photography in the Fine Arts.*

The mid 1960s brought two more Artmobiles which made a total of four. Recognizing this unique system and the calibre of the Museum Theatre, the National Endowment for the Arts in 1966 chose the museum as Virginia's administrator of a $50,000 matching grant for professional theatre. The money was used to circulate Museum Theatre productions throughout the Commonwealth.

Cheek in 1965 invited Virginia businesses to play a part in the museum's programs. Many firms responded and became patrons, helping to underwrite exhibitions and plays. The Corporate Patrons made up the museum's sixth support group, along with the museum trustees, the 12,000 museum members, the Collectors' Circle, the Council and The Fellows. Seldom had an art museum enjoyed such warm and widespread popular support. ☐

The architect's model for the proposed Entrance Wing at the north end of the Virginia Museum shows the portico, automobile approach road and sculpture garden.

CHAPTER XI

The Virginia Museum
HARVEST YEARS 1965-1968

January, 1966, Cheek at the Boulevard entrance sign for *Building for the Arts and Arts Unseen,* an exhibition which unveiled plans for the South and Entrance wings. Museum expansion was dictated by unprecedented growth in the state institution's collections and staff.

160

In November of 1967, Paul Mellon revealed to Leslie Cheek his intention to give the Virginia Museum a large number of French Impressionist paintings from his private collection. The board of trustees authorized preliminary designs for a Mellon Wing, to be located on the west side of the museum, to house these anticipated treasures. The plans, however, were shelved after color renderings had been made. This gift, which would ultimately include a large number of English paintings, drawings and watercolors, along with French post-Impressionist and Cubist masterpieces, would be finally displayed in a monumental West Wing eighteen years after Mellon first proposed making it.

Planning for the Mellon Wing was halted in 1967 because resources were already committed to building two other additions to the museum's aging and cramped quarters. A wealth of art gifts and acquisitions was descending on the museum. The years of Cheek pioneering—of creating exhibitions, developing an audience, and cultivating prospective donors—was paying off with many significant additions to the museum's collections.

Yet how could the museum adequately exhibit its new treasures? The success of Cheek's efforts by the 1960s now demanded more galleries, public rooms, storage and personnel. The staff of nineteen and the budget of $78,000 which Cheek found when he took over the museum in 1948, had grown in nearly twenty years to 139 people and to over $1 million yearly. The museum anticipated other potential gifts—particularly from the

Art Deco, Art Nouveau and American contemporary art collection of Sydney and Frances Lewis, creators of Best Products, with headquarters in Richmond.

With the success and health of the museum assured, Cheek decided to retire in 1964, but was prevailed upon to remain. In 1965 Cheek suggested to president Walter S. Robertson that he be permitted to turn over daily museum operations to an administrator. This would enable Cheek to devote full time to the museum's expanding programs, though he suggested he be paid only half his former salary. Robertson wanted Cheek to remain at the helm, and over lunch at Richmond's Commonwealth Club he agreed to the director's plan for changing the museum's administrative structure. William J. Rhodes, Jr., the museum's business manager, was named administrator. The new arrangement worked well through Cheek's retirement in 1968. Even so, Leslie was hard pressed to keep up with the museum's booming growth.

The most urgent demand was for space. To meet it, Cheek in 1965 proposed two additions to the building. One was a South Wing, affording architectural balance with the then-existing North Wing, which housed the theatre. With the aid of architect Robert Stewart of Richmond's Baskervill and Son, Cheek developed a plan for a new multi-story South Wing centering on an interior court in Italian Renaissance style, with surrounding galleries. Below the court on several levels were to be a new library, many offices and work spaces, and an Artmobile dock.

ABOVE: Librarian Betty Stacy in the South Wing's spacious library which opened in 1970. **BELOW:** The Renaissance Court was inspired by Italian designs.

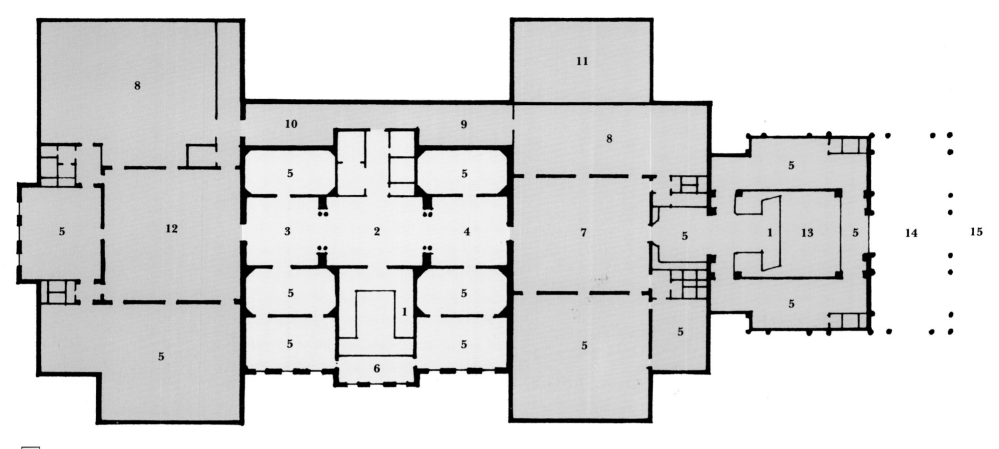

■	1936 ORIGINAL BUILDING
■	1955 NORTH WING
■	1970 SOUTH WING
■	PROPOSED NORTH WING

1	STAIRS	9	STORAGE
2	MAIN HALL	10	KITCHEN
3	SOUTH HALL	11	STAGE HOUSE
4	NORTH HALL	12	RENAISSANCE COURT
5	GALLERY	13	ENTRANCE HALL
6	BALCONY	14	PORTICO
7	MEDITERRANEAN COURT	15	SCULPTURE GARDEN
8	LOAN GALLERY		

LEFT: In each of fourteen galleries at the Virginia Museum were orientation theatres, seating ten, with automated slide shows presenting 14-minute art history lectures. In the Baroque Gallery, visitors entered the theatre through a stately 16th century Florentine doorway. The painting at left is Salvator Rosa's *The Death of Regulus*, purchased through The Williams Fund in 1959. **RIGHT:** The museum's French Gallery was dominated by this huge stone mantle measuring nearly twelve feet high. The 16th century piece once belonged to William Randolph Hearst, who at his death owned warehouses full of unused decorative objects. The paintings shown in this view are by Vignon, Poussin, Lorrain, Lancret, Greuze, Volaire and van Loo.

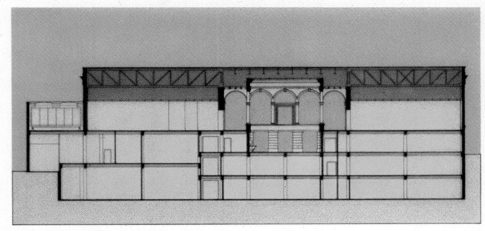

CROSS SECTION THROUGH SOUTH WING

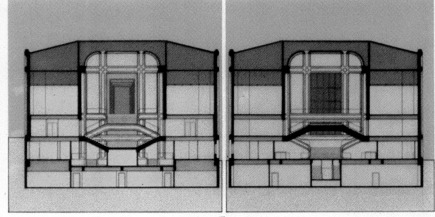

CROSS SECTIONS THROUGH NORTH WING

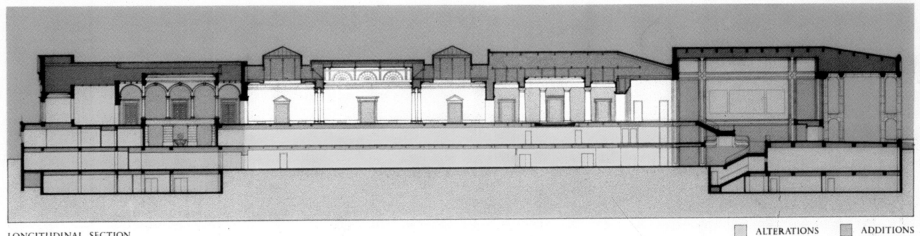

LONGITUDINAL SECTION

☐ ALTERATIONS   ☐ ADDITIONS

ABOVE: The shaded area in the section drawing of the South Wing (top left) shows the Renaissance Court, below which were the library and administrative offices. The section of the Entrance Wing (top right) depicts the grand Paris Opera stairway that was to be its centerpiece. The longitudinal section (below) shows the planned additions in relation to the 1936 structure at center. The idea was for visitors to walk along the length of the museum, encountering world cultures chronologically organized in galleries grouped around three courts: Renaissance, Mediterranean and Medieval. **RIGHT:** The portico to the proposed Entrance Wing would have overlooked the museum's sculpture garden.

The $3.5 million South Wing, begun in 1967 and opened three years later, eased museum operations. While planning for it was underway, Cheek and Stewart worked on designs for the more complicated Entrance Wing to be built adjacent to the North Wing. In young Robert Stewart, Cheek found a skilled architect whom the museum director had helped train in understanding museum problems. The two would collaborate on many other projects in the years to come. A native of North Carolina, Stewart had served as a summer intern with the Virginia Museum before earning his architectural degree at Yale.

Cheek's planning of the proposed Entrance Wing in the years 1965-67 was to prove the most time-consuming and disappointing chapter of his Virginia Museum tenure. From its start it posed problems, for it envisioned an imaginative new museum entrance, a soaring two-story entrance lobby, and an exterior façade which had to be carefully designed and landscaped to avoid detracting from the existing structure.

Cheek proposed a contemporary entrance to the museum with a large exterior portico. The rectangular building would attach to the existing North Wing by a neck, which would be screened along the Boulevard by trees and shrubs. Though its appearance would be in a more modern idiom than the Wren-styled museum building, the proposed new wing's materials and decorative features would relate closely to the older building.

Visitors approaching this new Entrance Wing by automobile would turn off the Boulevard into what appeared to be a tunnel but was actually an extended approach ramp to the portico at the new entrance. Openings along the south wall of this ramp allowed glimpses into the new formal garden, complete with sculptures, reflecting pools, and splashing waterfalls cascading down its three terraces. Bearing to the left, the motorist followed the ramp upward and arrived at the marble-floored portico. After dropping off passengers, the driver could either re-enter

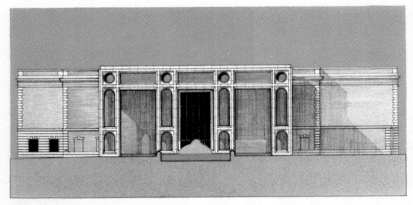

NORTH ELEVATION

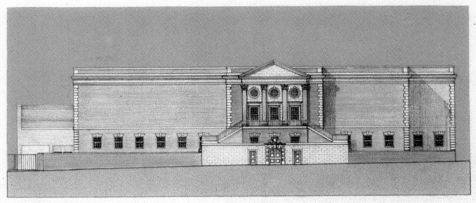

SOUTH ELEVATION

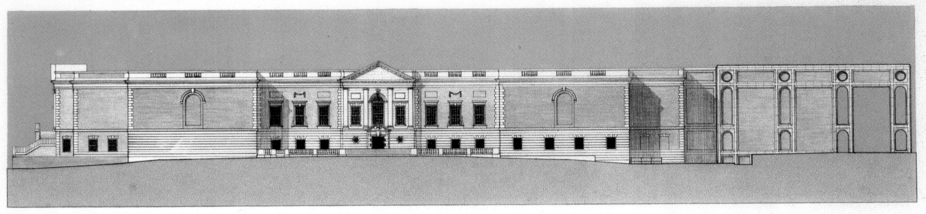

EAST ELEVATION

Elevations of the South and Entrance wings. The Virginia Art Commission refused to approve the Entrance Wing declaring that the addition was out of scale with the old headquarters building.

OPPOSITE PAGE: After leaving their cars at the portico, museum-goers would have stepped into this stair hall in the Entrance Wing. The room was designed to accommodate six huge 18th-century Gobelins tapestries.

the Boulevard, or follow another roadway leading around the garden to the parking area.

From the portico, museum visitors walked into the Entrance Hall which was centered on the museum's impressive long main axis. The hall introduced visitors to the museum's galleries and featured six large Gobelins tapestries. Via a grand "Paris Opera" stairway, museum-goers could ascend to the upper level galleries, or descend to the theatre lobby. On the lower level were also theatre offices and multipurpose public meeting rooms for art classes, art organizations and other museum programs.

As architect Stewart pointed out, one effect of relocating the museum's main entrance at the north end of the building would be to create a new longitudinal orientation for the visitor, who would be able to view the length of the museum's interior down a series of courts and halls, around which were situated the various galleries. The Boulevard entrance, used since 1936, would be closed, with the result that visitors arriving at the new Entrance Wing would be closer to the theatre, the galleries and the parking area.

Under the plan, the lower level of the earlier museum structure would be remodelled to contain a larger Members' Suite, plus a

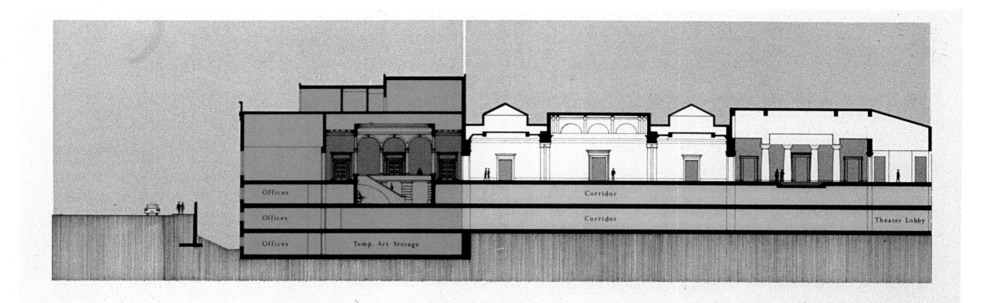

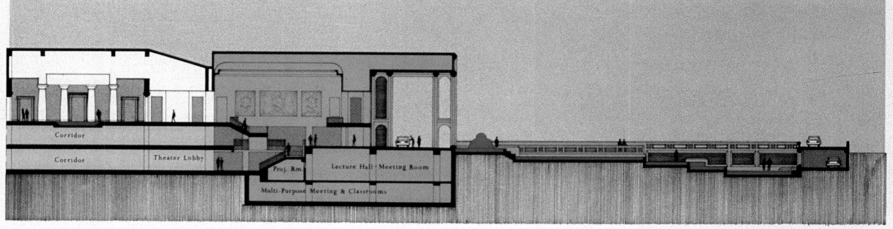

Offices

Offices

Offices · Temp. Art Storage

Corridor

Corridor

Theater Lobby

Corridor

Corridor · Theater Lobby

Proj. Rm. · Lecture Hall - Meeting Room

Multi-Purpose Meeting & Classrooms

Scale in feet 0 10 20 30 40 50

BASKERVILL & SON, ARCHITECTS

Cheek decided to put two levels of the South Wing (top) below street level to keep its roofline consistent with the 1936 building. The small structures topping this wing were to accommodate a television studio and guest rooms for visiting lecturers, but these facilities were never built. A stepped fountain (below) was at the center of the planned sculpture garden around which circled the Entrance Wing approach road.

visitors' cafeteria. After examining the plans, architect Wallace Harrison of New York concluded that Cheek and Stewart "have managed to capture the lively spirit of the museum and the contemporary society it services . . . It is one of the best solutions to this kind of problem I have seen."

Despite Cheek's best efforts, however, the State Art Commission objected to the proposed Entrance Wing design, calling its scale "inappropriate" in relation to the earlier building. The nine members of the commission, who were responsible for approving state-funded building projects, made their report to the governor. In an effort to overcome their objections, Cheek and Stewart thrice revised their plans, but without success. On its final examination in 1967, the Art Commission approved the revised interior layout, but continued to disapprove the exterior. Again, the museum's hopes for the new addition were dashed.

Faced with further discouraging delays, Cheek decided to go through with the resignation which Walter Robertson had previously persuaded him to withdraw. At a board of trustees meeting on February 28, 1967, he told president Erwin Will, Robertson's successor, that he wished to leave as soon as a new director could be found. However, Cheek and the board agreed not to make any public announcement until a successor had been found. Meanwhile, Cheek continued his planning role and an interim committee was organized to run the museum. Its members were administrator William Rhodes, curator Pinkney Near and programs director William Gaines.

While the public was unaware of these maneuverings, the museum flourished. In 1968 trustee Paul Mellon made possible the acquisition of 274 objects of Near Eastern art dating from 200 BC to 190 AD. The museum bought this collection for just under half a million dollars from Nasli Heeramaneck, a New York collector and dealer. It was exhibited as *The Arts of India and Nepal*, to be followed by another new and stunning acquisi-

The Arts of India and Nepal opened at the museum in September, 1967 and featured these significant additions to the museum's permanent collection, purchased from Nasli Heeramaneck of New York.

Adviser Marvin Ross helped the Virginia Museum build one of the country's best collections of Byzantine art. This 5th century B.C. bronze bust of Minerva was acquired in 1966 through The Glasgow Fund. Ross was but one of several advisers whom the museum retained during Cheek's twenty-year directorship.

LEFT: *Festival Designs by Inigo Jones* displayed costumes and scenery designs for Stuart masques by the 17th century English master. The show, which opened in January, 1968, was circulated by Washington's International Exhibition Foundation. **BELOW LEFT:** Opening in January, 1967, *William Hogarth* was up to that time the largest display ever assembled in the United States of the English artist's work. Included were 43 paintings, 52 prints and 15 drawings.

Homage to Rodin was the final Virginia Museum exhibition held under Cheek's directorship. Shortly after it opened in September, 1968, the museum acquired Rodin's *Study of a Woman's Torso,* a gift of B. Gerald Cantor.

tion, shown as *Byzantine Treasures*. The jewelry, stone sculptures, metalwork, coins and textiles were bought with museum funds on the advice of part-time adviser Marvin Ross, formerly of the Walters Gallery. The objects, dating from the 4th to the 12th centuries, comprise one of the best Byzantine collections in the nation.

Cheek's last two major exhibitions were *Festival Designs by Inigo Jones* and *Homage to Rodin*, both held in 1968. Inigo Jones' paintings and architectural designs were borrowed from the Duke of Devonshire's collection at Chatsworth, while most of the Rodin sculptures were loaned by the Los Angeles County Museum.

When the trustees encountered difficulty in finding Cheek's successor, he became impatient. In September of 1968—nineteen months after he had notified the board of his wish to retire—Cheek wrote president Will to say he would formally step down on October 31. In accepting Cheek's decision, Will called it an "immeasurable loss to the Virginia Museum, the state, and the entire art world." Will praised the out-going director for his lively programming which he declared had influenced museums everywhere. The board agreed to Cheek's appointment as "Director Emeritus."

The resignation, following Leslie's highly publicized career, was headlined in newspapers and art journals. Letters and phone calls deluged the director, begging him to stay on, but his mind was made up. He felt his life's work had been fulfilled.

In May of 1969, following a four-month Pacific cruise to the Orient, Cheek returned to Richmond to be honored at a testimonial dinner, planned by Helen S. Dohn, Cheek's secretary at the museum for over ten years. Politicians and leading figures from the art world joined with trustees and staff to hail Leslie and Mary Tyler. Director Perry Rathbone of the Boston Museum, an old friend of Cheek's since his days at Harvard, brought greetings. Justice Albertis S. Harrison, Jr., of the Virginia Supreme Court and a recent governor,

The end of an era: Leslie Cheek receives the Rhoads Medal from Walter S. Robertson during farewell dinner ceremonies at the Virginia Museum, May 16, 1969.

thanked Leslie for all Virginians whose lives he had enriched. Walter Robertson gave Cheek the museum's Webster Rhoads Medal for outstanding contributions to the arts. President Erwin Will presented the trustees' gift of a silver wine cooler.

And what of the future? Perry Rathbone at the museum dinner touched on it when he told guests that the Cheeks were building a retirement home on the Blue Ridge Parkway, overlooking the small town of Vesuvius. "I must ask," Rathbone added impishly, "is there a Pompeii below in the valley? Does it know what volcanic energy that mountain is now sheltering?" Then, as laughter subsided, he said, "As you and I know—and Leslie must surely sense—it is impossible for him to enjoy idling thoroughly unless he has plenty of work to do."

His twenty-year stewardship of the arts in Virginia had come to a close, but as Rathbone prophesied, Leslie was not one to sit still. There were new projects to undertake, a world to travel, and, most importantly, a mountain-top farm to run. ☐

Seated Scribe, Sema-tawy-tefnakht, Late Period (Saite) Dynasty, 664-610 B.C. The Williams Fund, 1951.

Stained Glass Window from Canterbury Cathedral, English 13th Century. The Williams Fund, 1969.

Bronze Ritual Vessel, Chinese 16th-11th Century, B.C. The Williams Fund, 1957.

170

Francesco Guardi, *Piazza San Marco,* Italian 18th Century. The Williams Fund, 1953.

Henry Moore, *Reclining Figure,* English 20th Century. The Glasgow Fund, 1962.

171

Pierre-Auguste Renoir, *Jeunes Filles Regardant un Album*,
French 19th century. The Williams Fund, 1953.

Don Quixote Tapestry, French 18th century, Gobelins Factory,
signed Audran. The Williams Fund, 1964.

Tosa Mitsunobu (attributed), *Pair of Folding Screens Depicting Birds, Animals and Flowers,* Japanese 16th century. The Glasgow Fund, 1966.

Athena Relief, Roman 1st Century A.D. (?). The Williams Fund, 1960.

Stuart Davis, *Little Giant Still Life,* American 20th century. The John Barton Payne Fund, 1950.

173

The "Jet Fountain" at the Cheek residence in Richmond.
(Photo by Richard Cheek)

CHAPTER XII

The Retirement Years

During the early years of Cheek's retirement, much of his time was absorbed with building his Blue Ridge Mountain retreat. Ever since he had parted with Faraway Farm in 1955, he had longed for another country place. Like Jefferson, he found his ideal spot in the Virginia uplands. "The high meadows of the Blue Ridge have always seemed to me among the most beautiful places on earth," Cheek wrote. The location was little more than two hours by car from their Richmond home.

The Cheeks had found this Shangri-La in 1966 after much searching. The 400-acre Fauber farm lay not far from the 1716 campsite of Governor Alexander Spottswood and his Knights of the Golden Horseshoe, overlooking the Valley of Virginia. Within the 360-degree view from the farm's highest point, one could see on a cloudless day into North Carolina and West Virginia. Narrow streams ran through the farm, gurgling through rhododendron and mountain laurel on their way to the Tye River in the valley far below.

At the first sight of the farm, Mary Tyler and Leslie both wanted it. "I think if we ever owned this farm I would die of joy," she said. She named it Skylark Farm.

Before he left the museum, Leslie concentrated on drawing plans for the place. He engaged Charlottesville architect Thomas Craven to prepare working drawings. The Cheeks spent hours stepping off the house site and dreaming of a complex of gray clapboard buildings with shingled roofs and fieldstone chimneys. He wanted Skylark to belong to the land, like the weathered Scotch-Irish houses and barns that motorists glimpsed through mountain mists as they traveled the Blue Ridge Parkway.

As the place for their house, Cheek chose the second highest point of the farm, called Round Top. It was 3,300 feet above sea level. There in 1969, a year after Leslie's retirement, ground was broken, and a road, well and septic field were built. Electricity and telephone lines were laid. Later, one of the streams on the property was dammed to create a pond for fishing and swimming. Building Skylark was not easy, for the contractor had to haul materials over a narrow road which looked down into a deep ravine.

Skylark was intended to be productive, and Cheek hired Lowell and Viola Humphreys of Nelson County to be its caretakers. Rather than growing grain or raising sheep, as

OPPOSITE PAGE: Skylark Farm, built by Leslie Cheek in the early 1970s. Located on the Blue Ridge Parkway near Vesuvius, Virginia, Skylark served as Cheek's retirement retreat for nearly a decade. Shown are the vehicle and equipment shed (left), the main house (center) and manager's house (right background). This picture was taken from what would have been the site of a four story "dream house," which was never built. (Photo by Richard Cheek)
ABOVE: Leslie Cheek, Jr., at Skylark Farm in 1978. Ill health forced him to give the farm to Washington and Lee University which now uses it as a conference center. The farm's upkeep is met through the sale of Christmas trees, raised there since 1966.

ABOVE: Skylark Farm as seen from the air. (Painting by William Bailey, Lynchburg, Virginia) **RIGHT:** From Skylark's highest point one can see three states. This view from the terrace (top) affords a sweeping view of the Blue Ridge Mountains. The living-dining room in the guest house at Skylark (center) with the Yardley screen, which Cheek purchased from the Virginia Museum, and two zinc boy and girl statues flanking the hearth. A picnic shelter (bottom) overlooks the pond and tennis court. Nearby is a nature trail winding through mountain laurel, dogwood, rhododendron and wild flowers.

did most of his neighbors, Leslie planted his hills with Fraser fir seedlings, which arborist Edward Gill of Virginia Polytechnic Institute had recommended as the most suitable for Christmas trees at the high elevation. Over the following decade Cheek was to establish ten large plantations of trees, each yielding firs of marketable size following up to twelve years of careful tending.

Leslie planned Skylark in two phases, the first to be built in 1969 and the second to come later. Phase One was a three-level manager's house, the top two floors of which the Cheek family would occupy until the main house could be built at a later date. Nearby were service buildings: a garage, an equipment shed with a small stable, and a flower and vegetable garden, enclosed to keep out rabbits. Fieldstone chimneys, forged iron hardware and a weathervane gave the house an early American look. At the pond, situated in a hollow a half mile from the house, Cheek built a picnic shelter and tennis court, with a trail leading through the woods near a trickling stream. The wildflowers which grew along this path delighted Mary Tyler.

Cheek and Tom Craven spent many months refining the elaborate design of the main house which Leslie hoped to build soon after the Phase One complex was completed. Phase Two was to be a four story residence reached through an underground automobile entrance drive. Leslie designed this unusual entrance to protect his family and guests from the winds which swept his mountaintop.

The three above-ground floors were arranged to embrace the far-spread view. The ground floor was given over to a comfortable family room around a wide fieldstone fireplace. The kitchen, servants' rooms and several childrens' rooms were nearby. The second floor was dominated by a library with floor-to-ceiling windows and by walls lined with Cheek's extensive collection of art books. On this level were also Leslie and Mary Tyler's suite, as well as bedrooms for their daughter Elizabeth and for guests. The third floor housed offices for Cheek and his secretary,

ABOVE: Robert Stewart's rendering of the never-built great house which Cheek planned for his mountaintop retreat. The oval wading pool was for the grandchildren. **RIGHT:** Entry to the house was had by an underground driveway. An elevator took guests to the living quarters on above-ground levels. Note the cascading waterfalls at right. Because of chilly mountain breezes, Cheek wanted to place the swimming pool in a below-ground gallery.

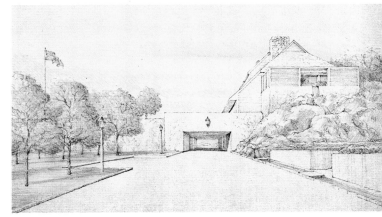

179

ABOVE: The 7-foot-tall portraits of Cheek's Warfield ancestors, painted in the 1850s, were to be hung in the library.
RIGHT: Cheek's grandchildren, Daniel and Julia play croquet on the upper lawn at Skylark. The great house would have overlooked this lawn, measuring over 250 feet in diameter, which is centered on the farm's second highest point, 3,300 feet above sea level. (Photo by Richard Cheek)

with an observation deck. An elevator served all four stories.

The south side of the house looked down toward the lower lawn with the pond and tennis court in the distance. The north side, with another spectacular view, opened onto a circular upper lawn that was nearly 250 feet in diameter. From the upper lawn grass ramps descended through terraced gardens to the Phase One complex of service buildings on the east side of the main house.

Cheek's taste for subtle architectural touches was evident in such details as his hexagonal garden toolhouse, topped by a cupola with a clock striking the time. On flagpoles near the parking court the hospitable family flew appropriate national, state, or college flags in honor of visitors. They added color and a bit of ceremony to weekends at Skylark, qualities Cheek relished in his life and work.

One day at Skylark, visiting Norfolk journalist Guy Friddell noticed Cheek's garden sentinel, which the family called Fearless Freddy. "The straw-filled scarecrow under a floppy hat is looking keenly over his right shoulder for marauding birds," Friddell observed. "Perched on his left shoulder is a saucy crow." Cheek had hoped Freddy would save his vegetable garden from hungry birds.

To simplify Skylark's housework, Cheek studied techniques which airlines had developed for quickly heating frozen meals with infra-red ovens. He designed rolling carts to whisk meals from kitchen to table. Meanwhile, in Richmond, the family continued to be served by brothers John and William Bradley, who had joined the Cheeks' household staff at Faraway Farm in the 1950s. Most of the family's help at Skylark was provided by the faithful Humphreys, especially in August, when Leslie III, Richard and Elizabeth, and their growing families, gathered on "the mountain."

The children had grown up and completed college by the time Skylark took form. After graduating from Harvard and later from Columbia, young Leslie III had tried journalism in Washington, but he switched to law after obtaining his degree at Georgetown. In time he became vice president of a trade association representing American insurance companies. His wife, Patricia Blake, is the daughter of Mary Tyler's lifelong friends Robert and Delia Carrington Blake.

Douglas, the second son, did not live to see Skylark finished. At twenty-three he died of Hodgkins Disease; a tragic loss of a young man of exceptional promise.

Richard Cheek, like his brothers a Harvardian, became a well-known architectural photographer with several books and many magazine articles to his credit. He married Elizabeth Upthegrove of St. Louis, and they make their home in Belmont, Massachusetts.

Elizabeth Tyler Cheek, the youngest child, studied art history at Winterthur and at Brown University after graduating in 1970 from Hollins College. At Winterthur, she met her future husband, Keith Morgan, who became an architectural historian on the faculty of Boston University.

Between them, the three Cheeks have seven children: Leslie and his wife, a daughter, Katherine, and two sons, Robert and Leslie IV, the latter an undergraduate at Harvard; Richard and his wife, a son, Daniel; and Elizabeth and her husband, a daughter, Julia, and twin sons, Will and Ned.

As they grew older, the three Cheek children reflected their parents' diverse interests. Leslie III, an optimistic extrovert like his mother, showed the orderly, businesslike instincts of his grandfather Cheek. Richard was imaginative and creative, like his parents, with an interest in architectural design. Elizabeth clearly had some of the Freeman gift for writing and speaking.

In 1974 Mary Tyler's mother died. Following Douglas Southall Freeman's death in 1953, Mrs. Freeman had moved to Richmond's Tuckahoe Apartments, where she spent her last years. There she shared in the pleasures of the nearby Cheeks, remaining active as long as her health permitted her in such roles as president of the Association for

Air view of the Stratford Hall Plantation reception center and Jesse Ball duPont Library. For many years Mary Tyler and Leslie have taken an active interest in the future of the Lees' ancestral home in Westmoreland County. This painting shows a gathering of the Stratford Hall Memorial Association's Directors on the library terrace. (Painting by William Bailey, Lynchburg, Virginia)

RIGHT: The parlor (top) in the Cheek guest house at Stratford, dedicated in 1981. It is used by guests of the Memorial Association. The information desk at the reception center (bottom), which houses a small Lee family museum and an auditorium with automated slide presentation about the historic plantation.

ABOVE: Robert Stewart's rendering of the reception center and footbridge which links it with Stratford's Great House. The deep ravine over which the bridge crosses was created in prehistoric times by the Potomac River. Cheek and Stewart's plans provided for future expansions at either end of the reception center, including a library, gift shop, restaurant and administrative offices. Thus far only the duPont Library has been built on this wooded site. **BELOW:** The Great House at Stratford Plantation, built between 1720-1730 by Thomas Lee. (Photo by Richard Cheek)

the Preservation of Virginia Antiquities.

With the children away, Mary Tyler was increasingly drawn into civic, educational and charitable causes. A Vassar classmate described her as "a blend of her mother's grace and her father's intellectuality." She became a trustee of Hollins and of the University of Richmond, where she and Leslie endowed a professorship to her father, a Richmond graduate and longtime University of Richmond board rector.

In 1975 Mary Tyler was elected president of the Robert E. Lee Memorial Association, whose 50 state directors guide the affairs of Stratford Hall, the grandly restored Westmoreland County birthplace of General Lee. Stratford became a shared passion of the Cheeks, helping fill the void left by Leslie's retirement.

He assisted in the planning of and helped pay for a discreetly modern expansion of Stratford's facilities, making possible the better handling of visitors and more research and teaching, dear to Mary Tyler's heart. Working with Robert Stewart, Leslie designed a Stratford Hall reception center given by Mrs. Eugene Stetson of New York, whose husband had guided the gallant band of ladies who saved Stratford. It included a small theatre for an orientation slide talk, plus a museum of the Lee family. Nearby is the Jessie Ball duPont Memorial Library with a broad exterior terrace for summer meetings and seminars. From this complex of buildings, visitors cross a footbridge to the Great House.

Cheek and Stewart also designed a guest house which was dedicated in the Cheeks' honor in 1981. Its living-dining room, kitchen and seven bedrooms are used mostly by guests of the Memorial Association's 50 directors, as well as by the men and women selected to attend the annual Stratford Summer Seminar for Teachers.

After Cheek retired from the museum, he missed the friends and the challenges of work he had left behind. Yet, with the help of Mrs. Dorothy Nielsen, who became his personal secretary in 1969, he stayed in touch

In retirement Leslie and Mary Tyler were constantly traveling. Fire walkers (top) on the Pacific island of Fiji prepare their incendiary path. A traffic jam (above) on a lake near Mexico City.

After retiring from the museum, Cheek and his wife boarded the *Kungsholm* for a Pacific cruise which retraced the travels of Captain Cook. During the voyage Leslie modeled his handmade Cook hat and telescope.

Mary Tyler at Peru's mist-enshrouded Machu Picchu in 1968. Later travels took the Cheeks to Africa, Hong Kong, Scandinavia, Europe and Japan. Leslie painstakingly planned each trip months in advance.

with the museum world, with his family, and attended to many requests for advice, architectural counsel and charitable gifts.

In retirement, Leslie limited his contact with people and events at the Virginia Museum. However, Leslie was pleased when the museum awarded him in 1977 a "Patron of the Arts" degree and medal. Two years later Governor John Dalton presented him with the "Bravo Award" at ceremonies for the first Governor's Awards for the Arts. In 1981 Cheek went back to the museum for "A Sentimental Evening," staged in his honor by the volunteer performers and stagehands from the early days of the Museum Theatre. Organized with infinite care by Jacqueline Viener and Meredith Scott, it recreated fragments from the hits of the 1950s and '60s. Among those participating were Mallory Freeman, Hansford Rowe and Robert Telford.

In 1985, the Virginia Society of the American Institute of Architects, in recognition of his contributions to the Commonwealth, awarded Cheek its Medal for Virginia Service.

Leslie continued to plan long cruises, which he and Mary Tyler took for months at a time, often as passengers on the Swedish-American Line's *Kungsholm* and *Gripsholm*. Wherever he traveled, Cheek continued to bombard his secretary with notes in his tiny script, while Mary Tyler kept a diary and wrote often to the children and to the household staff at Pocahontas Avenue and Skylark Farm. On their return, Leslie, after methodically filing hundreds of color slides, would write Richmond travel agent Willard Alley to thank him for his bookings and comment on the trip abroad.

Having always enjoyed exuberant good health, Leslie began in the 1970s to suffer

from weakness and dizziness. At first his disorder was diagnosed as Parkinson's disease, but doctors later concluded his affliction was the result of pressure produced by arthritic growths on his spinal cord. His condition worsened, and in 1978 he underwent painful back surgery in Philadelphia's Jefferson Medical College Hospital. The operation did not help. His difficulty in walking did not improve, and his sense of balance remained impaired. Though he was only seventy and otherwise vigorous, he faced the fact that he could never travel again.

Even though he was sidelined by illness, Leslie took vicarious pleasure in his wife's numerous civic activities. Despite the fact that his handwriting was made worse by his affliction, he continued to scrawl letters to friends and colleagues the world over, which Mrs. Nielsen neatly typed.

183

The Cheeks' home in Richmond's West End. Designed by Duncan Lee and completed in 1919, Leslie and Mary Tyler have lived here since 1948. Cheek has made numerous changes, including the addition of a swimming pool and pool house in the 1950s, and a jet fountain in 1983. In 1985 a glassed-in Galleria was constructed beneath the wisteria-covered loggia. In the late 1970s Leslie briefly contemplated donating the property to the Commonwealth of Virginia as a second Governor's Mansion, but the idea was dropped. (Painting by William Bailey, Lynchburg, Virginia)

ABOVE: Chauncey Ives' *Pandora* (which Cheek purchased from the Virginia Museum) graces the garden. In 1984 the grounds were open to the public for the first time for Virginia's Historic Garden Week. **LEFT:** The enclosed sun room (right) overlooks the shaded terrace where Cheek takes daily walks. (Photos by Richard Cheek)

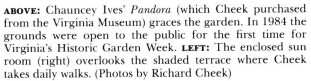

RIGHT: Scenes from Cheek's 75th birthday party, October 28, 1983. The portrait of President John Tyler in the dining room (top) honors one of Mary Tyler's ancestors. Guests arriving at the front door (center) pass gaily decorative arrangements of evergreens. Mary Tyler (bottom) dances with author G. Kidder Smith. The waiter's colorful sash is a Cheek trademark. (Photographs by Ronald Jennings)

Cheek receives the Bravo Award from then-Governor John Dalton at the First Governor's Awards for the Arts, 1979.

Cheek with Pamela and Carter Brown at William and Mary's Charter Day exercises, February, 1984.

Leslie Cheek, Jr., at his Richmond home. The Latin inscription over the pool house door, carved by son Douglas Cheek in 1959, translates "O joyful people entering, forget your cares." (Photo by Richard Cheek)

O · SOCII · INTRANTES
LAETI · DISPELLITE · CURAS

Cheek plans his days to accomplish work on his many continuing projects without rush. Always a fastidious and well-groomed man, he carefully dresses each morning. Because of impaired muscular control, he has designed special shirts and matching neckties which he can easily put on himself. Confined to his Richmond home and garden, he takes daily exercise and devotes himself to collecting flags and art books, and organizing his enormous collection of color slides. In the evenings, he watches television, or reads.

The many visitors to Pocahontas Avenue keep Leslie and Mary Tyler informed about the world. Mary Tyler's guests from Main Street, Church Hill and academia mingle with Leslie's friends from the arts. Cheek enjoys drawing up guest lists for birthday and Boxing Day parties. For these, he and designers Raymond Geary and William Ryan create imaginative invitations and floral decorations.

Leslie Cheek's illness made it impossible for him to build the long-dreamed-for main house at Skylark Farm as he had planned. Instead, in 1977 he and Mary Tyler gave the farm to Washington and Lee University in honor of Douglas Southall Freeman, whose award-winning biographies had helped the world know both of the school's namesakes. Today, Washington and Lee holds scholarly conferences, trustees' meetings and faculty gatherings at the picturesque retreat. As Cheek planned, profits from the sales of Christmas trees defray the farm's upkeep.

In 1982 Washington and Lee broke precedent and awarded honorary degrees to both Leslie and Mary Tyler. They were the first couple to have been so honored in the university's 233-year history.

Despite his recognition and his wealth, Cheek retains a lifelong shyness. His wife provides a comfortable buffer in groups of unfamiliar people. He has never truly enjoyed public speaking, even after dinner. He has an inborn naïveté which has never grown jaded, and his humor is never far below the surface, delighting in teasing and irreverent repartée.

"He's not effusive," says his neighbor and long-standing friend Mary Robertson, the widow of Walter Robertson. "If he likes a person, he will do anything in his power except be over-familiar. And if he doesn't like them, he doesn't." There is something appealingly courtly, old-fashioned and blunt about Leslie Cheek.

He was pleased in 1983 when Paul N. Perrot of the Smithsonian Institution was selected to be director of the Virginia Museum. With Perrot's leadership, he foresees the realization of some of his remaining dreams for the museum, which will celebrate its 50th anniversary with the opening of a $22 million West Wing in December 1985. Designed by Hardy Holtzman Pfeiffer Associates of New York, this magnificent wing, with walls of roseate Italian marble, was made possible through the generosity of Sydney and Frances Lewis, and Paul and Rachel Mellon. This handsomely designed addition will house portions of their gifts to the museum.

Next to the Virginia Museum, none of Cheek's life interests is closer to his heart than the Fine Arts Department at the College of William and Mary, which he initiated in the 1930s. He and Mary Tyler were pleased to contribute in 1983 to the building of the Muscarelle Museum of Art on the college's 300-year-old campus, and to advise its first director, the youthful and capable Glenn Lowry, before he was called away to the staff of the Freer Gallery in Washington.

When the museum was dedicated on William and Mary's annual Charter Day in February 1984, Leslie and Mary Tyler were among the honored guests. Cheek was clearly the hero of the day, especially after the principal speaker, J. Carter Brown, director of the National Gallery of Art, credited Cheek with "the modern rebirth of the fine arts at the college" and with influencing his own museum career. The crowd loudly applauded Cheek, who struggled from his chair and smiled in acknowledgement.

Afterward, Mary Tyler helped Leslie into their car for the drive back to Richmond. In Cheek's own life, the progression from teaching arts in Williamsburg to creating a great museum in Virginia had consumed most of his lifetime. They had been difficult years, but the rewards had been great. And who could foretell what other Cheek achievements lay ahead? □

Afterword

One unexpected pleasure involved in having attained the status of septuagenarian—at the moment of writing I am seventy-eight as opposed to Leslie Cheek's more modest seventy-seven—is that when you read a biography of one of your immediate contemporaries it takes on doubled interest as a biography, at secondhand, of yourself. I don't think there was a single date in Leslie Cheek's life as recounted here that I didn't compare with that date in my own life; my personal concordance would make up another book longer than this one. Where was I at such and such a time? What was I doing? How well did I know the other people involved in this or that incident of Leslie's life? Why, I wonder, did we never meet at Yale, where our attendance overlapped by three years, especially since I knew all the other students and staff mentioned in that part of Leslie's story.

Our backgrounds were different in early years—I a raw middle-westerner and Leslie a suave Southerner—but they gradually fused as I took on a degree of polish and Leslie allied himself with the movement of transforming art in this country from an amusement for the elite to an enrichment of the daily life of a community. We finally met as teachers while he was at William and Mary and I was at the University of Virginia. Our similar ideas about the state of art in America led him to his career as museum director and me to mine as art critic. During all those years we never entirely lost touch.

Looking back, then, with this kind of double vision, I realize that we began to grow toward our professions during years when art itself was still a kind of poor relation in American society. In our first youth art held at the very best the position of a kind of revered maiden aunt of aristocratic lineage, and as a corollary was frequently regarded with suspicion as a major interest for a normal male. I remember that in the 1920s when George Bellows emerged as a pre-eminent American painter, it was always emphasized in his press notices that he

was a boxing fan and had been an intercollegiate basketball champion. It was safe to like him.

Reading this biography, then, I realized that anyone who cannot remember clearly the turn of the 1920s into the '30s can have no idea of the transformation in the American art scene since then, a transformation brought about by museum directors of Leslie Cheek's perception. At the end of the jazz decade, art museums outside a few major centers were all but non-existent, and even in New York the Metropolitan was little more than a respectable provincial approximation of its European models. The Museum of Modern Art was just issuing from the womb, with modest quarters in an office building, and the National Gallery in Washington was not even an embryo.

I hope it is apparent to other readers of Leslie Cheek's story that his triumph lay to an exceptional degree in his creation of a union that is now taken for granted as basic to the successful operation of American art museums—the enlistment of the privileged few into the service of a wide general audience. It is worth noticing that the book opens with a description of the "glittering throng" (specifically an "invited" list) including the British and American ambassadors at the Sponsors' Dinner at the opening on the evening of April 2, 1960, of the exhibition *Sport and the Horse*—forms of sport with an aristocratic European lineage dear to the Virginia gentry. *Sport and the Horse* could very nearly serve as a summary of Leslie Cheek's goals as director of the Virginia Museum and his means of achieving them. The subject had a strong local interest, in line with his conviction that a Virginia museum should maintain roots in its home culture. At the same time, the exhibition carried no taint of provincialism, since interest in George Stubbs and similar English "horse painters" at that moment was raising them to international esteem and vastly increased historical stature. Also, this was an exhibition that everyone could enjoy: you didn't have to have your own racing stable, nor did you have to be an art historian or esthetician, to respond to these paintings—realistic renditions that in many cases evoked a storybook England. After enjoying an exhibition like this one, even the most timorous citizens would feel more at home in a museum that in other exhibitions would lead them into the mysteries of modern art.

I believe that at heart and in spirit Leslie Cheek was always a teacher, and like other first-rate teachers he knew that one of the most effective ways to present your ideas would be in disguise. He was a teacher of art—its esthetic principles, its reflection of social factors of its time, its capacity for telling us about ourselves by revealing unsuspected psychological aspects of the world around us. He was teaching the "glittering throng" as well as everybody else what art was all about. But in doing so—and this is important—he never presented art as a mystery that had to be approached with a long face or resort to hyperintellectual abacadabra. The definition of the function of art, which is "to enlarge, clarify, or intensify our experience," does not preclude the primary fact that art is a pleasure—a most profound pleasure. To have opened that pleasure to so many people, as Leslie Cheek has done, must surely be a profound satisfaction.

—JOHN CANADAY
New York

BIBLIOGRAPHY

MAGAZINES

The Architectural Forum, January, 1946
Life, 6 August 1945
Time, 6 April 1953; 19 October 1953; 13 May 1957; 25 April 1960
Newsweek, 26 October 1951
House Beautiful, June, 1951
Magazine of Art, March, 1938
Theatre Arts, May, 1951
Arts in Virginia, Fall, 1965
Southern Living, May, 1980
The New England Architect and Builder, January-February, 1934
Landscape Architecture, January, 1947
The Congressional Record, September, 1968
Architectural Record, April, 1940

MUSEUM PUBLICATIONS

Bulletin, Virginia Museum of Fine Arts
Annual Report of the Director, Virginia Museum of Fine Arts
News, Baltimore Museum of Art
Architecture in Virginia 1776-1958: The Old Dominion's Twelve Best Buildings
W. O'Neal, *Architecture in Virginia, An Official Guide to Four Centuries of Building in the Old Dominion*

EXHIBITION CATALOGUES

Baltimore Museum:
    A Century of Baltimore Collecting, 1940
    Scenery for Cinema, 1942
    Sculpture and Carl Milles, 1940

Virginia Museum:
    Sport and the Horse, 1960
    Healy's Sitters, 1952
    Design in Scandinavia, 1954
    Painting in England 1700-1850, 1963
    Treasures in America, 1961

BOOKS

Norman Newton, *Design on the Land: The Development of Landscape Architecture,* (Cambridge: Belknap, 1971).

Thomas Bergin, *Yale's Residential Colleges: The First Fifty Years,* (New Haven: Yale, 1983).

Carl Zibart, *Yesterday's Nashville,* (Miami: Seemann, 1976).

Martin Kaplan (ed.), *The Harvard Lampoon Centennial Celebration 1876-1973,* (Boston: Little, Brown, 1973).

Reuben Holden, *Yale: A Pictorial History,* (New Haven: Yale, 1967).

Aline Saarinen, *The Proud Possessors,* (New York: Random House, 1958).

David Stevens (ed.), *Ten Talents in the American Theatre,* (Norman: University of Oklahoma Press, 1957).

John Walker, *Self-Portrait with Donors: Confessions of an Art Collector,* (Boston: Little, Brown, 1969).

Meyric Rogers, *Carl Milles: An Interpretation of his Work,* (New Haven: Yale, 1940).

Education, Bricks, and Mortar: Harvard Buildings and their Contribution to the Advancement of Learning, (Cambridge: Harvard, 1949).

MISCELLANEOUS

Cheek Papers
Cheek Scrapbooks
Virginia Museum Directors' Files, Virginia State Library, Archives Division, Richmond, Virginia

INDEX

Page numbers in *italic* represent matter which is either mentioned in captions or is the subject of illustrations.